D1562544

Opinion Leadership

Opinion Leadership
The Power of Word-of-Mouth
Influence and Persuasion

Joel N. Greene, Ph.D.

Opinion Leadership: The Power of Word-of-Mouth Influence and Persuasion

ISBN-13: 978-1-7336319-3-8
Kindle/PDF: 978-1-7336319-2-1

Cover design by Luisito C. Pangilinan

Table of Contents

List of Figures

List of Tables

DEDICATION

I dedicate this book to the Opinion Leaders who changed my life:

Robert Weinberger
Charles Chrysler
Phil Gerst
Kenneth Marr
George Capuzello
John Estrella

—Joel N. Greene

PREFACE

Figure 1: "And Here There Be Dragons"

Old maps of uncharted seas often depicted unknown areas with such labels as, "And Here There Be Dragons." You entered these perilous regions at your own risk. The trouble was, you didn't know what, in actuality, was awaiting you: an island full of gold and riches, or perhaps nothing.

Organizational databases could echo a similar warning, "and here there be opinion leaders." While not perilous, this is a customer category that is largely uncharted. Although the databases contain large amounts of information, the identity of opinion leaders has been elusive for many years. There have been no charts or gps devices available to lead you to them easily.

Yet, opinion leaders offer the rewards of free word-of-mouth advertising! They can disseminate information to their peers, extolling the benefits of services or products and therefore impact sales positively.

Customers view opinion leaders as honest, objective, sincere and truthful sources of information and advice. The question is, how do you tap into this source of positive messages and endorsements? Up into now, this was no easy task. The current measures of opinion leadership are only correct about 50% of the time, the same probability as tossing a coin. You never know if you have identified the opinion leaders you want to reach.

The opinion leaders in your customer databases are "hidden in plain sight." Due to a lack of opinion leadership theory, and poor measurement instruments and methods, opinion leaders are virtually undetectable, and therefore not very useful in terms of reaching a customer base.

But now we have the means of identifying who opinion leaders are and how we can reach them. This book presents a comprehensive theory of opinion leadership – and a measurement approach -- which identifies opinion leaders according to several personality traits that opinion leaders characteristically have.

This book introduces the Personal Construct Theory of Opinion Leadership, the first theory of opinion leadership to show why opinion leaders feel compelled to offer information and give advice to others. It provides a theoretical framework for opinion leadership that is comprehensive enough to integrate the past research history of opinion leadership from its inception in the 1940s through today's contemporary scholarship. This includes an explanation of who online influencers are and how they differ fundamentally from opinion leaders.

The book also introduces a process measure of opinion leadership based on interpersonal communication behavior that can be used independently, either to identify opinion leaders or to validate opinion leaders found via the personality trait components of the opinion leadership theory. The book also introduces a new sociometric measure of opinion leadership, which also shows why traditional measurement approaches, which relied on memory and recall, are accurate only 50% of the time.

Along the way, this book debunks a number of myths and erroneous ideas about opinion leadership that have become deeply ingrained over the years. Here are several myths and their corrections:

	Myths	Reality
1	Opinion Leaders share many traits, but personality does not cause or drive opinion leadership behavior.	Opinion Leaders share cognitive personality and communication traits that enable and predispose them towards opinion leadership communication activity.
2	Opinion Leaders are People of Status, e.g., sports figures, politicians, celebrities, etc.	Opinion leaders are one's peers, e.g., family, friends, neighbors, and co-workers, etc.
3	Opinion Leaders tend to specialize in one topic or product area exclusively.	Opinion Leaders are not confined to one product or topic area; they can engage and influence people across diverse product or topic categories.
4	Opinion Leaders can be identified by self-report measures.	Observation of the Opinion Leader communication process is the most valid method of identifying Opinion Leaders. We can also predict the identity of Opinion Leaders by using specific personality traits.
5	Opinion Leaders exhibit high levels of product knowledge and interest.	Product knowledge and interest are unrelated to opinion leadership. Opinion Followers (non-leaders) reflect high levels of product knowledge and interest in order to compensate for skill deficiencies when they sometimes act as Opinion Leaders.

Table 1: Opinion Leadership Myths

The book also considers the migration of influencers onto the Internet in an effort to determine the role that they play in social media sites. This includes a review of studies that try to identify online Influencers based on their network location, display of influence, and information flow. Finally, the book explains how the Personal Construct Theory of Opinion Leadership applies to both offline opinion leadership situations, and to online Influencers and social media websites.

The author hopes that the Personal Construct Theory of Opinion Leadership and related measures will allow opinion leaders to be identified and understood much more readily, particularly in consumer databases. Hopefully, this book will lead to additional insights about interpersonal influence and encourage research and investigations into new and exciting areas of opinion leadership inquiry for many years to come.

ABOUT THE AUTHOR

Joel N. Greene, Ph.D. is a Direct Marketing consultant, educator, and sailor. He was Director of Database Marketing at Signet Jewelers Inc., the world's largest specialty retail jeweler, where he managed all customer analytics and targeting for some 12 retail brands and websites, including Kay Jewelers and Jared. Dr. Greene was Vice President of ABS Direct, serving many Wall Street clients including Citibank, Key Bank, Cyrus J. Lawrence, etc. Other clients have included AT&T, and the U.S. Departments of Commerce, Defense, and Energy. Dr. Greene has taught marketing as a full-time faculty member at Hofstra University, LIU and Manhattan College. His doctorate in Marketing is from the Graduate Center, City University of New York. Dr. Greene initially worked in the financial industry as a Trust Officer with Bankers Trust Company, New York.

Dr. Greene is also the author of *Direct Mail Marketing: What works? What doesn't work? How To know the difference!* which was a #1 New Release in Advertising on Amazon.

"Experience has shown that most advice comes from person to person"

Nathan of Breslov (1843), *Likutey Halakhot*

CHAPTER 1

THE FIVE OPINION LEADERS WE MEET ON EARTH

Among the many books that he's written, inspirational author, Mitch Albom, wrote a wonderful bestselling novel, *The Five People You Meet in Heaven.* I believe, if you are fortunate, you also get to meet at least five Opinion Leaders (perhaps more, perhaps less) in your own life while you are here on earth.

These Opinion Leaders essentially help prevent mistakes by steering you in the right direction about many things, some trivial, some perhaps even life changing. In looking over my own life, I realize that I've been lucky enough to have met some key people who were willing to share their advice and wisdom when I needed it. In effect, they were Opinion Leaders, and they helped me make choices about career, marriage, education, and other goals. I've dedicated this book to them.

Usually conversations with Opinion Leaders are about minor or routine things in life, and therefore go largely unnoticed. For example, some years ago, I bought a sailboat, having seen one I instantly fell in love with at a yacht club in Charleston, South Carolina. It was a brand-new Rhodes 22, a small but extremely well-equipped and versatile day sailor that had accommodations for a weekend or longer excursions. I don't think I've ever seen a boat as beautiful as this one.

Although I had once owned a 16-foot Nordica sailboat years earlier, I realized that I knew little about evaluating boats or how to pick a boat that would be right for me. I needed to find someone

Figure 2: The Author at the Helm of Prometheus

I could trust who could help me decide on which boat to buy. Fortunately, I mentioned my intention to buy a sailboat to someone I had recently met, Steve Mendoza. Steve was the owner of a large boat; he was also the Commander of the Beaufort Squadron of the America's Boating Club, and therefore knowledgeable about all things nautical. I told Steve about my plans, and he not only agreed with my purchase of *Prometheus*, a Rhodes 22 that I found for sale online, but he also did something quite extraordinary. He offered to drive us to Florida in his pickup truck and help me bring the boat and trailer back to South Carolina. I immediately and gratefully accepted his offer.

Opinion Leadership, as we shall see, is not only important to us individually, but it is of immense value to organizations, both large and small. In effect, opinion leaders appear to be disseminators of information, often about new products, political candidates, medical procedures, religious services, fashion choices, restaurants, educational institutions, real estate, gym memberships, movies, and tv shows; and the list goes on.

A satisfied customer, who is also an opinion leader, may influence friends and family via word-of-mouth about the products or services they purchase in the future. Since we often rely on the recommendations and advice from others, this word-of-mouth channel of influence is essentially a critical part of consumer and individual decision-making that can greatly benefit the bottom line of most organizations.

So, who are these opinion leaders, and how do we identify them? Although we may intuitively think that opinion leadership is easy to define and measure, it is actually one of the most elusive and frustrating concepts to fully grasp.

To answer the questions above, it's important that we understand how the concept of opinion leadership developed and to get grounded in its historic roots.

Historical Perspectives

John Stuart Mill is usually cited as the first person to describe those individuals whom we currently call, opinion leaders. In his book, *On Liberty,* published in 1859, Mill wrote that

> "the mass[es] do not now take their opinions from Dignitaries, in Church or State, from ostensible leaders, or from books. Their thinking is done for them *by men like themselves* [emphasis added], addressing them or speaking in their name, on the spur of the moment, through the newspapers."

There is an earlier mention of the word-of-mouth process that appears in the rabbinic literature. In his book, *Likutey Halakhot*, Rabbi Noson Sternhartz (Nathan of Breslov) in 1843 wrote that

> "experience has shown that most advice comes from person to person."

Since Mill goes deeper, and makes useful distinctions, we shall continue to refer to his definition.

Mill draws a key observation about opinion leaders and other individuals we usually call "celebrities" – those who garnish special attention from their office, athletic ability, etc. Mill notes that the general masses of people do not obtain their opinions from celebrities or other leaders or dignitaries in the community.

He emphasizes rather that one's opinions are shaped or influenced by peers and, therefore, not by individuals of higher status, fame nor fortune. People tend to seek the opinions of individuals they know and with whom they interact, such as family, friends, and co-workers. During the 1850s, it is one's peers who wrote in the newspapers, since newspapers and pamphlets were, like telephones today, a means that individuals employed to make their opinions known to others. That is why Mill distinguishes between newspapers and books.

Let's contrast Mill's quotation with a typical definition of opinion leader that appears on the Internet today:

> "An opinion leader is a well-known individual or organization that has the ability to influence public opinion on the subject matter for which the opinion leader is known. Opinion leaders can be politicians, business leaders, community leaders, journalists, educators, celebrities, and sports stars." (study.com, 2015).

John Stewart Mill would disagree. Opinion leaders were never meant to include public figures nor famous people. Accordingly, we will label movie stars, sports figures, and other public entities, along with individuals on digital platforms, such as bloggers on Instagram, and others with huge social media followings, as *Influencers*. Influencers are not opinion leaders, but represent different channels of communication and influence and, therefore, need to be differentiated and considered separately.

Let's consider one additional, key definition of Opinion Leadership, that is more in line with the Mill's earlier observations:

> "What we shall call opinion leadership, if we may call it leadership at all, is leadership at its simplest: it is casually exercised, sometimes unwitting and unbeknown, within the smallest grouping of friends, family members, and neighbors. It is not leadership on the high level of a Churchill, nor of a local politico, nor even of a local social elite. It is at quite the opposite extreme: it is the almost invisible, certainly inconspicuous, form of leadership at the person-to-person level of ordinary, intimate, informal, everyday contact. Our study is an attempt to locate and learn something about these everyday Influentials." (Katz & Lazarsfeld, 1955)

This definition was developed as part of the pioneering research studies conducted by Columbia University sociologists in the 1940s and 50s who coined the term "opinion leadership." In their view, as we can see, the opinion leader is someone whose influence involves those in close spatial and social proximity, e.g., face-to-face interactions with friends, neighbors, relatives, and co-workers. When we talk about opinion leadership or word-of-mouth influence, we are referring to the peer-to-peer exchanges of opinions, ideas, and news that occurs directly between individuals, or among groups, based on their interpersonal relationships.

The epicenter of the opinion leadership research was located at Columbia University and it produced two seminal works on the topic. The first, *The People's Choice* (1948) by Paul F. Lazarsfeld, Bernard Berelson, and Hazel Gaudet, studied the 1940 Presidential election with the objective of understanding how political opinions and attitudes are developed, formed and changed (Lazarsfeld et al, 1948). It was here that the importance of opinion leadership and personal influence were first identified within the context of political decisions and voting behavior.

The second publication appeared in 1955 under the title, *Personal Influence*. This work, by Elihu Katz and Paul F. Lazarsfeld (Katz & Lazarsfeld, 1955), described several additional studies of opinion leadership, including marketing leadership (food, household products, and consumer goods), fashion leadership (clothing, hairstyles, and cosmetics), public affairs leadership (political and social issues), and movie leadership (movie preferences and choice).

Notably, Jefferson Pooley (2006) has pointed out that the Katz & Lazarsfeld's opinion leadership studies greatly benefited from the insights and ideas gained from Edward Shils, a sociologist at the University of Chicago, about small group research and the resistance that masses often exhibit regarding mass media influence.

Personal Influence focused primarily on the structure and flow of information within the social system or network. For example, it replaced the generally accepted hypodermic needle or contagion theory in which the mass media largely impacted everyone in the audience equally and at the same time (see Fig. 3).

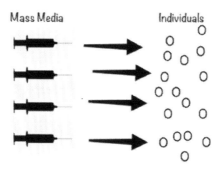

Figure 3: Hypodermic Needle Model

The researchers postulated a new, two-step flow theory which suggested that opinion leaders first received information from mass media, and then disseminated that information to opinion followers (see Fig. 4).

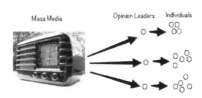

Figure 4: Two-Step Flow Hypothesis

The structural network analysis gave birth to the use of sociograms to map the social links within social systems, in which group members could be identified as those who influence others and act as opinion leaders. To help determine the directional flow of information, participants are often asked to maintain social episode diaries to record interactions with others with whom they interact. Here is a typical sociogram involving several households in a study of buyer perceptions of hybrid automobiles:

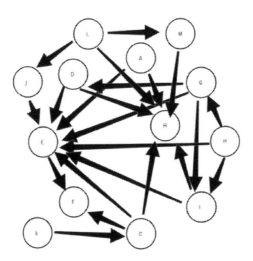

Figure 5: Sociogram of Hybrid Automobile Discussions

Operationally, we can simply count the number of information requests (or arrows) received by each group member, ranking their order them from highest to lowest, and thus determine who acted as the opinion leader(s). In this social network (Fig. 5), it appears that there are two opinion leaders, "E" whose opinion is sought by seven individuals, and "H", whose advice is sought by six individuals.

In recent years, using sociograms has become increasingly popular in the analysis of online information flows within social media networks (Choi, 2015; Watts & Dodds, 2007).

Knowledge & Interest

Katz & Lazarsfeld (1955) tried to determine if the influence of opinion leaders was limited to one area of interest, or whether a multiple topic opinion leader or *"general leader"* type existed. They found little support for the existence of "a generalized leader" in their study, and concluded that "each arena it seems, has a corps of leaders of its own."

Other researchers have similarly addressed the issue of product specificity over the years by examining the overlap of opinion leadership across topics and products. For example, King and Summers (1970) studied opinion leadership across a variety of product categories and reported that the greatest overlap occurred in related areas (e.g., large and small appliances). Researchers have noted similar findings for innovators. In a study of opinion leadership across 10 topic areas (e.g., household furnishings, appliances, home cleaning and upkeep, recreation and travel, politics, children's behavior and upbringing, women's clothing and fashion, family medical care, cosmetics and personal care, cooking, recipes and new foods, and automobiles), Myers and Robertson (1972) and Marcus & Bauer (1964) also found evidence of overlap within related product areas.

Given this evidence of limited overlap in related areas, the consensus among researchers has been that opinion leaders have an interest in one topical area (such as medical procedures, political candidates, food products, fashion, cosmetics, etc.). By acquiring greater knowledge about a topic, it is generally believed that the extent of opinion leader influence over others seeking their advice and guidance may be limited to specific areas of interest. We shall address this view in more detail in chapter nine.

Personality Traits & Related Characteristics

There have also been attempts to determine if opinion leaders share common personality traits (such as gregariousness, agreeableness, etc.), demographics (such as age, income level, marital status), or sociological indicators, (such as degree of social mobility), compared to non-leaders.

Overall, researchers have found a large number of characteristics that correlate directly with opinion leaders. These characteristics include greater reading interests, more self-confidence, and financial conservatism, self-reliance, gregariousness and narcissism, brand loyalty, inner-directedness, social involvement, age, education, income and occupation, media usage, and product knowledge and interest.

Perceived risk, first conceptualized by Bauer (1960), has also received attention as a variable that may be associated with opinion leadership.

Bauer (1960) suggested that

> "one of the very important functions of opinion leaders is to reduce the perceived risk of the behavior in question."

Research has shown that-word-of-mouth activity helps to reduce perceived risk for new products and for products that may involve financial or other social consequences when a poor decision is made (Ross, 1975).

Perceived risk has been viewed either as an inherent personality trait (individuals having high-risk levels), as a function of a demographics such as age (being risk-averse due to limited resources), or as a function of product class (high-ticket items). In each case, opinion leaders may help to assuage the level of risk inherent in the purchase decision.

Other researchers have approached the identity of the opinion leader by specifically considering the product or object category associated with specific groups of opinion leaders. The category of fashion opinion leadership is a notable example of this type of product-related research (Kim, 2011). Other product or service-related studies have also considered opinion leaders who purchased new automobiles, energy conservators, service users, family planning clients, and romance novel readers. Many of these studies view opinion leadership as a product-specific phenomenon rather than as a general personality trait.

Some studies have also considered the identity of opinion leaders within different consumer markets or segments, and lifestyles, e.g., farm owners, entrepreneurs, and elderly consumers.

From a practical, and a theoretical standpoint, the above dimensions (e.g., personality traits, product class, demographics, sociological characteristics, etc.) have provided researchers with little help in explaining or predicting opinion leadership communication behavior.

Katz & Lazarsfeld also suggested using three social dimensions, e.g., gregariousness, life-cycle position, and social status, as one possible means of differentiating opinion leaders from non-leaders within network systems. Table 2 shows some general definitions of these terms.

Social Dimensions	Definitions
Life-Cycle	One's progresion in life indicated by age, marital status, number of children, etc.
Gregariousness	The number of relationships and interations one has with others within a network
Social/Economic Status	Determined by one's educational level, cost of housing, etc.

Table 2: Social Characteristics
(Based on Katz & Lazarsfeld, 1955)

The researchers suggested that the three social dimensions would be related to opinion leadership, enabling individuals to act as opinion leaders within society and within social networks.

According to the results in Table 3, lifecycle performed well in three out of the four opinion leadership areas. Gregariousness and social status appeared to be largely unrelated to opinion leadership.

	Marketing	Fashion	Public Affairs	Movie-Going
Life-Cycle	High	High	None	High
Gregariousness	Moderate	Low	Moderate	None
Social Status	None	Low	Moderate	None

Table 3: Significance of Social Dimensions
(Based on Katz & Lazarsfeld, 1955)

The researchers realized that the lack of significance in comparing individuals thought to be opinion leaders versus non-leaders might be caused by an underlying problem. Either these variables were actually unrelated to opinion leadership, or else the subjects were too similar across the dimensions being measured.

Katz & Lazarsfeld specifically raise the latter possibility in a footnote about women opinion leaders, when they cautioned against

> "making the tacit assumption that leaders who are 'cosmopolitan,' or 'highly interested,' or 'very gregarious,' etc. are also going to be influential for others who are very much less cosmopolitan, or much less gregarious than themselves....It is much more warranted to assume that opinion leaders influence women of their own groups --- women who are very much like themselves. Thus, it is important...to determine in what ways opinion leaders differ from the close associates whom they influence." (Katz & Lazarsfeld, 1955).

In this book, we suggest that the difficulty of ascertaining differences among opinion leaders and non-leaders stems from far more serious problems than variable selection or subject similarity. As discussed in the next section, several research problems have plagued the opinion leadership arena since its inception.

Research Issues

The first issue concerns the measurement approach that Katz & Lazarsfeld, and other researchers, have used to identify opinion leaders.

In the People's Choice, Lazarsfeld et al (1948) indicated that the researchers identified opinion leaders by asking a panel of participants these two questions (during the 1940 Presidential campaign):

> "Have you tried to convince anyone of your political ideas recently?"

> "Has anyone asked your advice on a political question recently?"

Those who answered yes to either, or both, questions were labeled opinion leaders. Lazarsfeld et al (1948) called this a "self-detecting" method, with the individuals identifying themselves as opinion leaders. These questions were later included in opinion leadership scales for easier administration as self-designating survey instruments (Childers, 1986; Rogers & Cartano, 1962; King & Summers, 1970).

Researchers also use a second approach, in which they identify individuals deemed to be experts, e.g., well-informed network members (or key informants) who are knowledgeable about group dynamics and group roles. These individuals are asked to identify specific individuals who act as opinion leaders within the network.

Over the years, the objectivity and impartiality of key informants have been questioned, since they might select opinion leaders to gain social standing or achieve some other agenda (Brooker & Houston, 1976; Nicosia, 1964).

A third method, called the sociometric approach, identifies opinion leaders by mapping the direction and flow of network influence. In this case, network participants are asked to identify individuals who influenced them, as well as members whom they influenced. By contacting the members within the network, the researchers can track those members who influence others within the network.

Although Katz & Lazarsfeld (1955) expressed the belief that the conversations reported by participants were "recent and recollectable," they felt it necessary to assess the accuracy of the information being recalled during subsequent interviews. Here's the result of their follow-up interviews:

> "Some of the advisers or advisees could not recall the specific conversation; others recalled topics different from the designated one; others were simply unable to recall whether the conversation had or had not taken place; and in a few cases, the 'designatees' completely denied having talked to the respondent about the specific topic" (Katz & Lazarsfeld, 1955).

The researchers indicated that they received confirmations in about 2/3 of the cases. They suggest this level of accuracy is sufficient, given there are no comparable studies with which to compare the results, and given the exploratory nature of the research being conducted.

The questions used, however, suggest the existence of some weaknesses in the measurement process. As Thomas Kuhn said, "the answers you get depend on the questions you ask." The validity of the data you get also depends on how you ask the questions. We should be apprehensive about the use of self-report or self-designating research questions when asking about a process or activity, such as the content of conversations that took place in the past. These methods rely on the participant's potentially faulty memory and ability to recall conversations in which their opinions were sought. Such questions are quite vulnerable to inaccuracies and faulty memories.

Rogers (1976) notes that

> "Diffusion researchers usually have relied on their respondents' ability to recall their date of awareness or adoption of a new idea. Essentially, the respondent is asked to look back over the shoulder to reconstruct his past history of innovation experiences. This hindsight is not very accurate and undoubtedly varies on the basis of (1) the innovation's salience to the respondents; (2) the length of time over which recall is requested; and (3) individual differences in education, mental ability, etc."

Self-report and self-designating approaches persist as the primary methods being used today to identify opinion leaders and non-leaders. Self-report Opinion Leadership Scales, such as the Childers (1986) scale, include self-assessment questions of as to whether the individual recalls influencing others or was influenced by them.

Researchers have suggested that the existing measures of opinion leadership may be reporting impressions of behavior, rather than the actual behavior itself (Brooker & Houston, 1976). The three techniques for identifying opinion leaders appear to rely either on the subjects' perceptions of themselves (overstating their socially acceptable roles as opinion leaders) or their perceptions of others. Perceptions of past behavior may also be distorted, and they may even reflect interactions that never occurred (Katz & Lazarsfeld, 1955).

Traditionally, there is a fourth method of measuring opinion leadership that is extremely accurate and effective. This method is called, "observation," and it entails actually observing (and/or recording) conversations as they occur among opinion leaders and non-leaders and then analyzing those exchanges to confirm the roles played by the participants. In the past, the observation method has been listed in the opinion leadership literature but apparently has been rarely used. Belk (1971) came closest to using the observation method in a study of opinion leaders in which subjects actively engaged in product related conversations. However, the conversations were only recalled by the subjects and were not directly observed nor recorded by the researchers.

The major difficulty with using observation is that it is extremely time-consuming. While self-administered surveys or opinion leadership scales can be completed within hours (and automatically collected and tabulated online), observations of numerous groups (of six to eight participants each) must be done in person and can, therefore, involves days or weeks of data collection and analysis.

Using observation entails assembling individuals to meet together as groups (perhaps using focus group facilities), determining the topics of discussion in advance (product purchases, for example), setting up recording systems, transcribing each group's conversation, and devising a means of analyzing and scoring the conversations once they have been recorded. This can be costly and may require additional resources, time, and effort.

It is somewhat disturbing to note that observation is no longer cited as a method of measuring opinion leadership in recent articles about opinion leadership (Chaudhry, 2013). The authors of one of the nation's leading consumer behavior textbooks have also discontinued any discussion of the observation method as a means of measuring opinion leadership in the latest edition of their textbook (Schiffman, 2019).

One of the major purposes of this book is to demonstrate why observation is the most reliable means of identifying opinion leaders. (Dear reader, please feel free to read that sentence again!).

We will provide a comparison of opinion leadership measurement methods to show conclusively that the results of self-report methods are widely divergent and inaccurate.

This book questions the efficacy of using the typical self-report opinion leadership scales employed by researchers. We believe that a reliance on self-report scales, that ask subjects to recall past conversations with others, is somewhat like using "a bent ruler." The same survey instruments may yield consistent results, however, they may not, in fact, be measuring the phenomenon in question.

In this book, we examine opinion leadership using the observation of actual word-of-mouth interactions. Based on the recordings and analyses of these conversations, we describe the use of a process measure of opinion leadership that can identify opinion leaders and non-leaders within groups of participants.

In Chapter Two, we address the most critical opinion leadership problem that exists today: the lack of an opinion leadership theory! By remedying this situation, we can identify opinion leaders quite easily, and we will also discover a means of predicting who they are in advance!

Summary

This chapter has defined opinion leaders as individuals who disseminate information and advice to other people who are usually in close proximity to themselves (family, friends, co-workers, etc.). Celebrities are not opinion leaders. Instead, we will label movie stars, sports figures, and other public entities, along with individuals on digital platforms, such as bloggers on Instagram, and others with huge social media followings, as *Influencers*.

The term, opinion leadership, was coined in *The People's Choice* (1948, 1960) by Lazarsfeld, Berelson, and Gaudet and in *Personal Influence* (1955) by Katz & Lazarsfeld. Similar ideas were articulated a hundred years earlier by John Stuart Mill (1856) in *On Liberty,* and in the rabbinic literature by Rabbi Nathan Sternhartz (1843), in his book, *Likutey Halakhot.*

Identifying Opinion leaders is elusive due to several research problems: the use of self-designating surveys which rely on memory and recall; and key informants who may be biased.

Despite being the most valid method of identifying opinion leaders, observation is rarely mentioned by consumer behavior experts. In fact, this method no longer appears in some of the leading consumer behavior texts, and it is similarly absent in a number of current research articles.

Action Steps

The following questions use part of the opinion leader self-designating scale shown below.

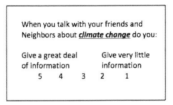

Figure 6: Opinion Leadership Scale Question

1. How would you personally answer the question, using climate change as the topic of interest? Do you ever act as an opinion leader regarding other topic areas or products? Why do you think that is so?

2. Please choose two friends and ask them to answer the question above about climate change. Did anyone indicate that they would act as a climate change opinion

leader? Ask your two friends if they are opinion leaders in any other area?

3. Based on your experience and knowledge of your friends, did anyone indicate that they are a climate change opinion leader when they would clearly not be? Do you agree with their answers? Why do you think they answered that way?

4. What have you learned from this exercise?

CHAPTER 2

TOWARDS A THEORY OF OPINION LEADERSHIP

"All truth passes through three stages.
First, it is ridiculed.
Second, it is violently opposed.
Third, it is accepted as being self-evident."
Arthur Schopenhauer, 1788-1860

Theories play various important roles. A theory provides a look at the "big picture," and thus helps us devise a workable blueprint for action, which makes having it incredibly beneficial and advantageous. For example, the Copernican Theory, explaining the movement of the planets around the Sun, is essential in telling us how to navigate safely over large distances and oceans.

Theories also show us how things fit together and offer explanations of phenomena not understood previously. Robert Koch's Theory of Germs guided Louis Pasteur's discoveries which prevented germs from invading the body and causing disease.

Well-accepted theories represent our best idea of what truth is at the present moment. Over time, we become attached to our perceptions of reality and they tend to become deep-rooted societally and impervious to change. Most people value stability, not uncertainty (Healy, 2018).

Paradigm shifts cause considerable distress by replacing old, hallowed approaches with new theories. According to Schopenhauer, society fiercely resists such change. The replacement process may take up to 20 years, about the life of a generation (Kuhn, 1962, 2015; Healy, 2018).

According to Kurt Lewin, "there is nothing as practical as a good theory" (Lewin, 1945). To understand the practicality and general value of a theory, as Lewin asserts, let's look at an example of an age-old puzzle, called the Elevator Problem, as depicted in Fig. 7.

Figure 7: The Elevator Problem

The problem involves a 24-floor office building in New York City that has but one elevator serving the building's 96 commercial tenants and customers. For some time, the tenants and their customers have complained about the interminable delays and sluggish operation of the elevator – a problem that seems to get worse. Several tenants have even threatened to break their leases and move out of the building.

The building's owner has hired an architect to devise a solution to the problem. After assessing the situation, the architect reports that another elevator could be installed in the building, at a cost of $2 million.

During lunch the next day, the owner tells a good friend about the trouble with his elevator and the costly solution he faces. The friend, who is a psychologist, offers to look into the situation and provide another objective opinion.

After a few days, the psychologist calls the building owner and announces that he can also solve the problem, but at a cost of $3,500. The owner is astounded and asks, "how can that be?

The psychologist replies, "well, let's just say that I'm a magician and that I can do it all with mirrors!" The next day, he has large, floor-to-ceiling length mirrors installed in the lobby, and on each floor, on the walls adjacent to the elevator.

As a result, the tenants and their customers are now happy, and they no longer complain about a slow elevator. At this point, you might also ask, "how can that be?"

It all boils down to how you define the problem and the theoretical framework you use to solve it. Here, the first solution defined the theoretical problem as part of physics concerned with physical matter and its motion through space and time. Another elevator was needed to move people more efficiently and in less time from one floor to another.

The alternative solution – mirrors – uses an altogether different theory or frame of reference, e.g., psychology. Psychologists focus on addressing how people function socially and emotionally in given situations. In this case, the psychologist realized that mirrors would allow people to view the objects they loved the most: themselves! By engaging them in this enjoyable manner, the building's visitors became self-absorbed and engaged with their reflections, so they no longer noticed any elevator delays.

Units of Analysis

Notably, Katz & Lazarsfeld, and their colleagues were a group of remarkable sociologists, whose research philosophy is reflected in the types of influence flow models or metaphors that were diagrammed at the time (sociograms, contagion theory, hypodermic needle models, two-step flow models, etc.). Their aim was to understand the exchange of influence and information at a "macro" or societal and network level, rather than at the individual's psychological level. They were less interested in understanding the motivations of the individual.

Indeed, we noted earlier that when Katz & Lazarsfeld used gregariousness, lifecycle, and social status, in an attempt to identify opinion leaders and non-leaders, they viewed those dimensions as "social characteristics." The opinion leadership phenomena were, therefore, explained according to sociological theory, as well as using survey and self-designating measurement methods, which often provide an ethnographic view of a society which focuses on its culture and customs.

Said another way, the units of analysis, used by Katz & Lazarsfeld and their colleagues at Columbia University, involved collectives or networks structures, while the units of analysis in most marketing and psychological studies, would be the individual and his/her cognitive and emotional characteristics and reactions. Despite the great achievements of the original opinion leadership research teams, the sociological models of opinion leadership have, over time, limited our theoretical frameworks. The result? For many years, we've been installing elevators rather than mirrors.

Over time, research about word-of-mouth influence and opinion leadership has shifted from sociology to other disciplines, including marketing, medicine, politics, urban policy, social media, etc. In addition, the focus of opinion leadership study also transitioned towards the need to identify personality dimensions associated with individual opinion leaders.

Personality Traits

Mostly, contemporary opinion leadership research has attempted to identify the key personality traits needed to understand opinion leadership behavior. Researchers try to understand the configuration of personality traits that enable individuals to act as opinion leaders.

Personality traits are internal psychological characteristics that are relatively stable and consistent over time, and that govern one's behavior, mannerisms and predispositions (Schiffman, 2019). They are also thought to have a biological or genetic origin which may, in part, reflect inherited abilities (Goleman, 1986). It's been observed, for example, that family members across several generations share trait attributes, such as musical talent, mathematical ability, intellect, and proneness to anger (Horvath, 1998).

The personality traits that have been linked to opinion leadership over time include extroversion, conscientiousness, agreeableness, openness, individuation, broad-mindedness, innovativeness, trust, involvement, influence, self-confidence, assertiveness, dominance, sociability, gregariousness, tolerance, and flexibility, among others. Many of these traits have an intuitive appeal and seem logical candidates for an association with opinion leadership.

The major obstacle to formulating a comprehensive opinion leadership theory has been the inability to integrate these diverse personality traits into a comprehensive model that explains and/or predicts opinion leadership behavior (Brett & Kernaleguen, 1975). Although positive correlations of personality traits and opinion leadership have been observed in numerous research studies, no "driving force" has been discovered among past trait analyses to explain why opinion leaders behave the way they do. In addition, these traits have been largely unsuccessful as predictors of opinion leader identities (Robertson & Myers, 1967).

Despite many investigations of these traits and various suggested opinion leadership models, a theory of opinion leadership, based on personality traits, has failed to materialize (Beatty, 1998). Thus, we continue to lack a psychological or marketing theory that can explain and predict opinion leader identities and explain why certain individuals act as opinion leaders.

Research studies often report partial correlations with respect to some opinion leadership traits, but not others. When such data varies from opinion leadership in some particular way, it may be claimed as a discovery of a new specific area of influence. Notably, the research literature contains a proliferation of influential agents who appear similar to opinion leaders, yet who are different in some other fashion.

- Influentials
- Key Influentials
- E-fluentials
- Hyperinfluentials
- Catalysts
- Information Sharers
- Information Brokers
- Product Champions
- Market Mavens
- Change Agents
- Social Leaders
- Authority Figures
- Persuaders
- Survivors

Figure 8: Proliferation of Opinion Leader Labels

In Fig. 8, for example, we see various labels applied to opinion-like leaders who disseminate information and knowledge, including those who were "thought" to differ from opinion leaders in some particular way.

What causes this proliferation in terminology? Without a doubt, research about opinion leadership is both fragmented and impeded by a lack of a commonly accepted opinion leadership theory.

Notably, Watts & Dodds (2007) made a similar observation:

> "Although the notion of opinion leadership seems clear, precisely how the influence of opinion leaders over their "immediate environment" shapes opinions and trends across entire communities or even a country, is not specified by the two-step flow model itself."

They note that although Kelly et al (1991) suggested that a framework explaining the role of opinion leaders in the population could be found in the diffusion of innovation theory, Watts & Dodds (2007), concluded that "on closer inspection, however, the diffusion of innovation literature does not specify any such theory." Despite thousands of articles and research studies about opinion leadership, a comprehensive theory of the subject has not been promulgated.

With the absence of a theory, is it any wonder that a multiplicity of opinion leadership typologies exists? A lack of theory exacerbates the problems in opinion leadership research by introducing a cohort of confusing and contradictory definitions and terms.

There is a compelling need for a new paradigm of opinion leadership to:

- Integrate and shed light on past research findings,
- Clarify current problems and issues,
- Point to new areas of research and development,
- Provide a practical, theory-based method of identifying opinion leaders,
- Increase the rates of diffusion and adoption of new technology, innovations or ideas; and
- Delineate how future opinion leaders could disseminate information more effectively.

There have been numerous attempts over the years to theorize or depict opinion leaders via visual models or frameworks. The next section reviews several of these attempts, along with a critique of their theoretical and practical adequacy. Are past models descriptive (which describe phenomena but do not predict or determine cause and effect) or are the models normative (explaining how/when/why opinion leadership behavior occurs)?

Earlier Conceptual Models

Many models of opinion leadership have attempted to describe the frequency and directional flow of interpersonal word-of-mouth communications. The simple two-step opinion leadership models show opinion leaders disseminating information directly to their followers, while "multi-step" opinion leadership models may add other information flows, including groups of followers who also receive information from media sources and from individual opinion leaders.

Notably, the two-stage information flow model, proposed by Katz & Lazarsfeld (1955), has seen a resurgence in recent years with the growing popularity of Internet social media sites, such as Twitter and Instagram (Choi, 2014; Watts & Dodds, 2007). In a recent article on the subject, Sujin Choi (2014) points out that online opinion leaders gain, in stature and in social influence, each time someone retweets their comments (also see Alfarhoud, 2017; Ho et al, 2016).

Some models have emphasized opinion leadership roles according to the prevalence of either giving or seeking information. They have labeled participants within a communications exchange as "discussers" (who discuss products, but who neither seek nor give advice), "mixers" (who both give and seek advice), and "silenters," who avoid such discussions (Gross, 1971).

Other researchers have defined opinion leadership as a dichotomy encompassing separate behavioral categories, e.g., "dynamic leaders" who disseminate information, versus "information exchangers," who engage in greater information sharing behavior (Tigert & Arnold, 1971). The latter categories advance the idea that information flows may not be unidirectional in that senders and receivers both exchange and internalize (e.g., encode or decode) messages during information exchanges.

Models of Social Engagement

One model that received considerable attention in the past was developed by Reynolds & Darden (1971). Their model depicts four categories of opinion leadership: the "socially integrated" who are high in both information giving and seeking; the "socially independent," who are high in information giving and low in information seeking; the "socially dependent," who are low in information giving and high in information seeking; and the "socially isolated" who are low in both information giving and seeking (Fig. 9).

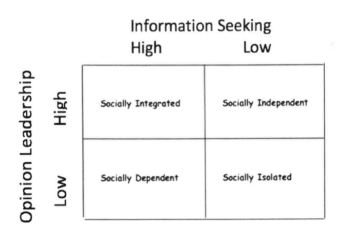

*Figure 9: Socially Integrated Communication Model
(Based on Darden & Reynolds, 1971)*

Although other researchers increased the number of categories (March & Tebbutt, 1977), the Reynolds & Darden (1971) model is important because it focuses on social integration as a possible cause of opinion leadership activity.

In another study, Darden & Reynolds (1970) also view opinion leadership as a social phenomenon and suggest that we may understand opinion leaders by analyzing their social connections. The researchers hypothesized that those who were inclined to be more active socially would be more active in exchanging information.

Prior to Darden & Reynolds (1970), the majority of models were primarily descriptive, not causal. The models sought to describe information flows and label participants, but they did not examine the causes of such behavior.

Models Based on Personality Traits

Opinion leadership models have also used a variety of personality traits and related psychological states to model opinion leadership activity. The following model (Fig. 10) is one example using involvement as a predictor of opinion leadership. Within the consumer behavior literature, involvement is viewed as a state of heightened motivation or arousal indicative of concern or engagement (Cai, 2004). In this case, it is depicted as a motivator of word-of-mouth activity.

The model suggests that involvement motivates the opinion leader to gain a substantial amount of product knowledge in order to engage in information sharing and influence within their area of interest (Venkatraman, 1990).

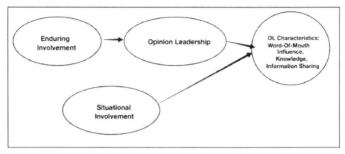

Figure 10: An Involvement Model of Opinion Leadership
(Based on Venkatraman, 1990 and Richens & Root-Shaffer, 1988)

Thus, the model suggests that opinion leadership depends on both knowledge and involvement being present.

Two European researchers, Gnambs & Batinic (2012), attempted to apply a universal or general trait-based personality model (using openness, conscientiousness, extroversion, and agreeableness), to predict generalized and domain-specific opinion leadership.

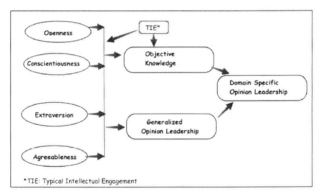

Figure 11: A Trait-Based Model of Opinion Leadership
(Adapted from Gnambs & Batinic, 2012)

The model above (Fig. 11) also included a variable abbreviated as "TIE," or typical intellectual engagement, which describes "differences in the effort an individual invests in engaging with new topics and the acquisition of new knowledge." In this model, Gnambs & Batinic (2012) suggest that TIE increases the opinion leader's level of involvement and knowledge within their specific domain of influence.

Although the model highlights the importance of the opinion leader's intellectual development, as a means of acquiring product knowledge, the cognitive components have not been linked to the communication abilities of opinion leaders. Instead, the model defines greater product knowledge as the principal criterion for the existence of opinion leadership.

Grewal et al (2000) developed a model of opinion leadership (shown in Fig. 12) using structural equation modeling (LISREL 8.12) to explore the question of whether one's social identity (identity derived from group membership) would be stronger for new, exciting products than for older, more familiar products (cars vs. computers).

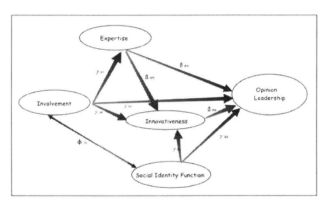

Figure 12: LISREL Structural Model of Opinion Leadership
(Based on Grewal et al, 2000)

The researchers found the social identity was strongly related to opinion leadership for cars, but not for computers. In addition, innovativeness was positively correlated with opinion leadership for cars (based on a self-designating scale), while expertise was positively correlated with opinion leadership for computers.

One would expect that situational variables could alter the results of this study. For example, if the participants were from an information technology (IT) group, a different set of results might be expected (e.g., such as a positive correlation between social identity and computer products or brands).

Notably, none of the models considered above provide any insight into our fundamental questions: why do certain individuals feel called upon to disseminate information to others? And, how do opinion leaders differ from non-leaders?

The next section focuses on a new theory of opinion leadership. Hopefully, this new theory will answer the questions of why opinion leaders play such a pivotal role in persuading and convincing other individuals about their decisions, including their product purchases.

The Personal Construct Theory of Opinion Leadership

This book introduces a new theory of opinion leadership as illustrated in Fig. 13. The Personal Construct Theory of Opinion Leadership is a comprehensive, integrated theoretical framework based on cognitive personality theory and opinion leadership communication behavior.

This chapter will explain how The Personal Construct Theory of Opinion Leadership explains the tendency and ability of opinion leaders to engage in persuasive and influential word-of-mouth communication behavior.

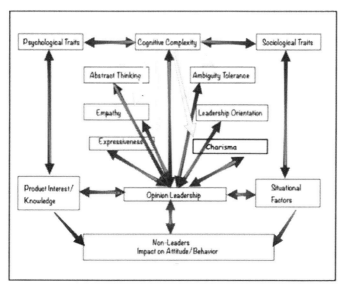

Figure 13: The Personal Construct Theory of Opinion Leadership

Although the traits in the proposed theory are independent, they are also linked theoretically as important parts of the opinion leader's personality structure. A relatively small number of traits, therefore, are required in this model because they represent the social and cognitive DNA of the opinion leadership personality. In this respect, the model also meets several other theoretical aims that make the use of a cognitive trait-based personality model feasible.

Specifically, The Personal Construct Theory of Opinion Leadership provides a linkage between communicator traits, cognitive functions, and neurobiological functioning. It identifies, as roots of opinion leadership, the cognitive and communication traits that are of critical importance in understanding opinion leadership behavior.

In addition, the model adheres to the requirements suggested in Beatty's (1998) standards for trait research. The model reduces an extremely large and diverse pool of communicator traits into a smaller, more parsimonious set of seven characteristics (e.g., cognitive complexity, abstract thinking, empathy, expressiveness, ambiguity tolerance, leadership orientation, and charisma). It can be evaluated for its adequacy according to its "internal consistency, testability, predictive power, explanatory scope, parsimony and elegance, empirical relevance, i.e. consistency with known facts," and its ability to provide "a sense of understanding about the phenomenon of interest," e.g., opinion leadership (Beatty, 1998).

Since the model is personality based, it also challenges whether opinion leaders are restricted to a specific product area, or whether they can, in fact, exert influence across diverse product categories. Similarly, the model addresses whether opinion leaders have greater amounts of product knowledge and interest than opinion followers, a topic discussed in chapter nine.

In addition, the model enhances one's ability to predict the identity of opinion leaders (and non-leaders) based on the traits associated with interpersonal communications. Finally, the model is robust enough to explore situations in which trait-based communication tendencies are absent or are suppressed, yet where opinion leaders still emerge within group settings.

At its core, this book introduces the relationship of cognitive complexity to other model variables and behaviors within a comprehensive theory of opinion leadership communication behavior. The Personal Construct Theory of Opinion Leadership, presented in this book, explains the changing landscape of interpersonal communication, such as the proliferation and dissemination of information in social media websites by Influencers.

The book demonstrates how the Personal Construct Theory of Opinion Leadership can be used by organizations, both large and small, to predict the identity of opinion leaders within customer databases, so that the organizations can interact more effectively and proactively with them.

Cognitive Complexity

Cognitive complexity occupies a central role in the Personal Construct Theory of Opinion Leadership.

Within the field of marketing, cognitive complexity has been used to assess the complexity of a consumer's mental condition or aptitude. Specifically, cognitive complexity measures the number of cognitive dimensions that consumers use to evaluate external objects and people. In marketing, these would include product and service dimensions, brand image, retail store personalities, company attributes and profiles, and advertising copy platforms.

Some marketers have studied the differences in cognitive structures as a means of segmenting consumer markets by discerning differences in product familiarity, assessing the degree of liking or disliking of products, and by determining the use of different consumer decision rules for purchasing products.

It's been observed, for example, that some (cognitively simple) consumers may only use two or three dimensions to evaluate a new product, while other consumers may use five to ten dimensions to assess the use and/or personal relevance of a product. The latter consumers (who are cognitively complex) would perceive and process a greater amount of quantitative information about a new offer. Such individuals would also process more qualitative information, particularly about different features and benefits that the product might provide.

Unfortunately, marketers over the years have largely disregarded the qualitative insights associated with cognitively complex thinking. In applying personal constructs to retail stores, for example, Hudson (1974), suggests that different cognitive complexity scores,

> "while indicative of definite interpersonal variations, are simply descriptive measures which reveal nothing about the content of these constructs. Nor do they reveal anything as

to the processes which give rise to these interpersonal variations."

The statement reflects a perception that cognitive complexity measures yield only descriptive or nominal (simple) data. Such studies use cognitive complexity as a methodological or operational procedure, ignoring the construct's broader theoretical implications. In short, such studies have failed to view cognitive complexity as a personality dimension which links the construct to interpersonal communication and other behaviors.

Other studies, however, have attempted to determine how cognitive complexity might be related to other consumer proficiencies. For example, one study investigated the relationship between cognitive complexity and product awareness, product knowledge and product consumption (Tan & Dolich, 1979). Although the results of this study were non-significant, the researchers noted that cognitive complexity has been treated as a personality characteristic in psychology. They argued that cognitive complexity appeared to be generalizable and may be capable of shedding light on various buying situations.

Cognitive complexity has also been studied with respect to consumer perceptions of intangible service attributes (Hirschman, 1981). The results indicated that users familiar with particular services relied on more cognitive components in their purchase decisions than did inexperienced consumers.

Researchers have also looked at cognitive complexity and the consumer's perception of products and company attributes. Durand (1978) found an inverse relationship between cognitive complexity and "halo error" – a tendency to view products superficially or simplistically. Durand found that cognitively complex individuals were more accurate in discriminating among different brands of dental products and automobiles than were cognitively simple subjects.

In a study about the comprehension of technical and complex advertising copy, researchers found that the recall and understanding of advertising messages appeared greater for cognitively complex individuals. To improve advertising effectiveness, the study recommended matching advertising copy with the cognitive ability of its targeted market audience (Zinkham & Martin, 1981).

Researchers have also focused on the behavioral implications of cognitively complex decision-making processes. In one study using financial services, the researchers found that cognitively complex consumers relied on their own opinions in making brand decisions, while less complex consumers followed the advice of significant others (Durant & Arie, 1980).

These findings are similar to studies in psychology where cognitively simple individuals have been found to depend more on external sources for information and guidance. We believe these findings also apply to opinion leadership in that non-leaders exhibit a tendency to look to others for advice and validation.

Cardinal Personality Traits

Personality is generally viewed as a pattern of characteristics that are stable over time and which largely affect one's long-term nature and behavior. Within this framework, cognitive complexity represents a key personality trait that determines how individuals usually think about and interact with objects (and people) in their environment. Due to its importance, cognitive complexity can be categorized as a cardinal trait, according to Allport's (1937, 1960, 1961) typology of personality traits.

According to Allport (1937),

> "In every personality, there are traits of major significance and traits of minor significance. Occasionally some trait is so pervasive and so outstanding in a life that it deserves to be

called the cardinal trait. It is so dominant that there are few activities that cannot be traced directly or indirectly to its influence…such a master quality has sometimes been called the eminent trait, the ruling passion, the master-sentiment, or the radix of life."

Allport (1937) notes that cardinal traits are not identical to the personality itself.

He writes, for example, that

"However well integrated a life may be around the cardinal trait there remain specific habits, incidental and non-organized tendencies, and minor traits of some degree that cannot be subsumed functionally under the cardinal trait. Though pervasive and pivotal, a cardinal trait still remains within the personality; it never coincides with it."

The view of cognitive complexity as a cardinal trait is consistent with the importance of *cognitive or mental structure* which Allport (1961) describes as the "key to the edifice of personality."

Cognitive complexity was developed as part of a Personal Construct Theory of Personality by two American psychologists, George Kelly (1955) and James Bieri (1955). It was formulated to explain how individuals formulate and use mental constructs to think and relate to others, as well as assess and react to external issues and objects in their environment.

The conceptualizations and operationalizations of Kelly's and Bieri's approach to cognitive personality theory focus on the nature and number of personal constructs that individuals use to describe other individuals.

The personal constructs or dimensions one uses develop largely from past interpersonal relationships. The quantity and configuration of personal constructs provide the individual with an ability to understand his or her social and physical environments (Bieri & Blacker, 1956; Wepman & Heine, 1971).

Cognitive Complexity and Opinion Leadership

A few studies have observed a relationship between cognitive ability and opinion leadership. For example, Brett and Kernaleguen (1975) suggested that an analysis of cognitive or perceptual styles might help to identify opinion leaders.

Childers (1986) observed that the opinion leaders of electronic and technological products acquired a considerable amount of consumption-related expertise. Unfortunately, Childers' thought this expertise enabled opinion leaders to use less cognitive effort in acquiring similar items.

Another study theorized a probable relationship among fashion opinion leadership, innovativeness, ambiguity tolerance, and cognitive complexity. Similar to Childers' viewpoint, they hypothesized that fashion opinion leaders would be cognitively simple due to a need for social conformity (Lennon & Davis, 1987).

A study by Reingen & Kiernan (1986), noted the possibility of a relationship between cognition and word-of-mouth ability. The authors suggested that future researchers should consider whether word-of-mouth activity is affected by one's cognitive perception of other people within one's network. Since the study focused on network flows of information, it did not investigate the suggestion further. The same researchers implied that research at the individual opinion leader level would be inadequate since it ignores the impact of the social or relational networks in which word-of-mouth communication occurs.

Richmond (1977) is the first study to demonstrate a theoretical and empirical linkage between cognitive complexity and opinion leadership. She found that subjects who were classified via self-reporting scales as opinion leaders appeared to expose themselves to more information. More importantly, subjects high in opinion leadership gained more than twice the amount of information than did subjects who appeared low in opinion leadership.

Richmond (1977) concluded that opinion leaders engaged in more complex cognitive processing than did non-opinion leaders. The opinion leaders were able to process and integrate a greater amount of information than non-leaders.

Richmond's findings are consistent with earlier observations by Bieri & Blacker (1956) that individuals appeared to be cognitively complex when considering both familiar and unfamiliar objects (e.g., inkblots vs. people). Although researchers usually posit there is a relationship between opinion leadership and product knowledge (in a known product domain), most studies do not test to see if opinion leaders score as high in product knowledge with unfamiliar objects. The lack of comparison between familiar and unfamiliar objects in many research studies obscures the role of product knowledge which may be fundamentally different in the cognitive thinking styles of opinion leaders vs. non-leaders.

Although Richmond (1977) did not consider the communication behavior of opinion leaders, her study represents a research milestone of tremendous value regarding opinion leadership.

A great deal of additional research has focused on differences between cognitively complex and cognitively simple individuals. Such differences have been noted with respect to the level of abstraction of mental concepts or constructs used by the individual, the capacity for ambiguity tolerance, the extent of empathetic communication skill, one's susceptibility to new information, the changeability of existing attitudes, and the use of internal (self-generated benchmarks) versus external referents (such as, seeking approval from others).

The studies of cognitive complexity reveal that personal constructs (e.g., their quantity and complexity) affect the individual's ability to perceive and interact with external phenomena (Bieri et al, 1966). Differences in individual personalities and dispositions arise from differences in mental structures and information processing competencies.

The cognitively simple person is viewed as having an elementary, less developed structure which restricts the individual to using a limited amount of information in narrow ways. In contrast, the cognitively complex individual is viewed as having a more mature or developed cognitive structure, allowing for the performance of more elaborate and intricate mental manipulations of larger amounts of information (Gardner & Schoen, 1962; Schroder et al, 1967; Bartunek, et al, 1983).

Using more information about external stimuli means that the individual uses a more multidimensional or complex style of thinking. They can develop a more complete mental perception or understanding of other individuals and objects. In contrast, cognitively simple people are characterized as using a limited number of personal constructs or mental descriptors to observe and describe external stimuli.

Cognitive Complexity & Communication

The existence of complex mental structures appears applicable to a fundamental area of opinion leadership: interpersonal communication.

Empirical research in the communications field has focused on the ability of cognitively complex individuals to engage in interpersonal communication. Delia, Clark & Switzer (1979) suggest that cognitively complex individuals can be viewed as "interpersonal behavior specialists" whose conversations reflect self-disclosure and interest in their immediate situations. Cognitively simple individuals appear to avoid such involvement.

In describing cognitively complex people, Delia, Clark & Switzer (1979) also suggest that cognitively complex individuals would have a predisposition to engage in interpersonal communication. Moreover, the researchers observe that

> "it appears reasonable to assume that interest in other people as an aspect of one's world leads to, and is developed in, interactions which may be characterized as 'participant centered.'"

Kelly (1955) and other researchers have theorized that the individual's cognitive system affects the characteristic ways the individual interacts with others within the external environment. It's also been suggested that the individual's cognitive system not only affects the way in which the individual interprets external information but also how the individual responds to others with respect to the individual's outgoing transmissions or communications (Zajonc, 1960, 1968).

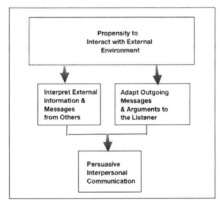

Figure 14: Cognitively Complex Communications System

Cognitively complex individuals tend to be sensitive to perceived listener needs, are more willing to disclose personally relevant information, and are more adaptable to formulate persuasive messages and arguments (Alvy, 1973; Hale & Delia, 1976).

Since the use of a large number of constructs improves the individual's understanding of external phenomena, the cognitively complex individual may comprehend more features and benefits of new products than do other consumers. The cognitively complex individual would be likely to discover areas of personal relevance in new product information, which presumably would be undetected by less complex individuals.

On this basis, the cognitively complex person may obtain a greater understanding of the features and benefits of a new product than would cognitively simple individuals. Researchers suggest the cognitively complex person may evidence a considerable degree of product interest and knowledge, factors deemed necessary in distinguishing opinion leaders from non-leaders (Montgomery & Silk, 1970; Myers & Robertson, 1972).

The propensity to gather and exchange product related information would also appear applicable to opinion leadership behavior. The ability to utilize multiple dimensions suggests that the cognitively complex individual would also have an ability to call upon a broad base of information in communicating messages with other consumers and offering advice which influences their purchase behaviors (Hale & Delia, 1976). Multidimensional thinking, the ability to distinguish different characteristics in objects or people, would also appear relevant to the opinion leaders' ability to communicate effectively with different audiences.

Assessing Levels of Cognitive Complexity

Cognitive complexity, as described by Bieri (1955), reflects a quantitative view of mental structure, e.g., the number and organization of constructs used by the individual's cognitive system, which are described as either complex or simple. The individual's level of cognitive complexity reflects the number of dimensions that one uses to understand external events and objects.

Cognitive complexity provides the individual with a multidimensional cognitive system that allows them to make a quick overview of situations, and comprehend the emotional nuances associated with various decision-making situations, including the purchase of new products, selection of healthcare providers, perception of political issues, and voting behavior, etc.

The three most frequently used measures of cognitive complexity include Bieri's (1955) Role Repertory Test, Scott's (1962) Sorting Procedure, and Crockett's (1965) Eight Role Category Questionnaire.

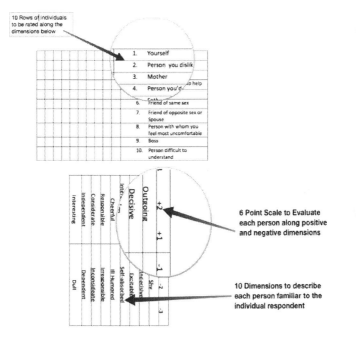

Figure 15: Bieri Rep Test of Cognitive Complexity

The Bieri Grid or Rep Test is the most straight forward measurement technique that uses predefined objects, which are easily recorded and tabulated (Fransella & Bannister, 1977). Fig. 15 provides an example of a Bieri Grid, with an explanation of how it is constructed, completed by respondents, and interpreted by researchers regarding each respondent's level of cognitive complexity.

One study, that compared several measures of cognitive complexity, reported that Bieri's was also the most adequate overall measure in terms of statistical validity (Vannoy, 1965). In addition, other methods of assessing cognitive complexity levels appear to be based on Bieri's approach, and they may introduce embellishments that are unnecessary.

To measure cognitive complexity levels, respondents would be given a 10 x 10 grid, with rows of representing individuals whom they find meaningful. Descriptive adjectives in the columns appear as scaled items ranging from +3 to -3. The respondents then rate each of the ten persons on all 10 dimensions.

For example, an individual rated on the first dimension, "outgoing-shy" would receive a numerical score from "+3" very outgoing to "-3" very shy, or anywhere in between. The level of the respondent's cognitive complexity is determined by matching object scores for each pair of rows. Here are Rep Grids completed by two individuals: using the +3 to -3 scale:

+2, +2, +1, -1, +1, +3, -3, +1, -3, +2
+1, -3, +2, +3, +2, -2, -1, +3, +1, +2
+3, +3, +1, +1, +2, +2, -3, +2, -3,+2
+1, -3, +3, +2, +2, -2, -2, +2, +3, +2
+2, +3, -1, -1, -1, +3, +3, +1, -3, +1
+2, -3, +2, +2, +2, +1, +1, +1, +2,+2
+1, -1, +2, +2, +2, -2, -3, +1, +2, +1
+2, -2, +2, +2, +2, -2, -3, +1, +3, +2
-1, -2, +2, +2, +2, -2, -1, +2, +3, +2
+2, -3, +3, +2, +2, -1, -3, +2, +3,+2

Subject #1

+2, +3, +2, -1, -2, +2, +2, +2, -2, +2
-1, -3, +2, +3, +2, +2, +2, +3, -2, +2
+3, -3, +1, -3, +2, +1, -1, +1, +2, +2
+2, +1, +1, +3, +3, +2, -3, +2, -3, +2
+1, -3, +1, +3, +2, +2, +2, -1, -1, -1
+1, +1, +1, +2, +2, +2, -3, +3, -2, -2
+1, -1, +3, -3, -2, -1, +2, -3, +1, +2,
+1, -2, -3, +3, +2, +2, +3, +1, -1, -2
+1, +2, +3, +3, -2, -2, +3, +1, -2, -3
+2, =3, -1, +2, -2, +2, =1, -2, =1, +3

Subject #2

Figure 16: Row Matches for Bieri Grids

If the respondent has differentiated the objects a great deal with respect to these dimensions, there would be fewer matches indicating a high level of cognitive complexity. A subject evidencing many matches is someone who differentiates to a lesser degree.

With a 10 x 10 grid, there are 45-row comparisons. The scores can range from a total of 450 (matches) which indicates a cognitively simple person who rated all persons or objects the same. A cognitively complex person would achieve a lower score, such as 125, indicative of a higher degree of differentiation among the objects or persons described in the grid.

```
Rows 1-2=1, 2-3=2, 3-4=3, 4-5= 0, 5-6=2, 6-7=5, 7-8=6, 8-9=8, 9-10=4   31
Rows 1-3=4, 2-4=4  3-5=2  4-6=4   5-7=2  6-8=6  7-9=4   8-10=6         32
Rows 1-4=1  2-5=0  3-6=2  4-7=4   5-8=2  6-9=5  7-10=3                 17
Rows 1-5=5  2-6=3  3-7=2  4-8=5   5-9=0  6-10=5                        20
Rows 1-6=3  2-7=4  3-8=3  4-9=6   5-10=1                               17
Rows 1-7=2  2-8=4  3-9=6  4-10=7                                       19
Rows 1-8=4  2-9=5  3-10=4                                              13
Rows 1-9= 1 2-10=3                                                     12
Rows 1-10=3                                                            3

                                                                      164
```

Figure 17: Bieri Grid Score for Respondent #1

As shown, in Fig. 17, the Bieri Grid score for subject #1 is 164. The individual shows low number of matches for a 10 x 10 grid, indicative of cognitive complexity. This cognitive structure aligns with the communication dimensions associated with opinion leadership. This person's cognitive structure would provide a tendency for them to communicate effectively and influence those around them.

An individual possessing a low Bieri score evidences a cognitive structure that allows them to compile and integrate a large amount of external information. At the same time, they can discern object differences and focus on the relevant attributes of individual stimuli. The individual's cognitive structure also involves a tendency to provide information verbally to other people who seek their recommendations.

Computing Bieri grid scores manually is rather time-consuming and tedious. There are several computer programs available through the internet that compute Bieri grid scores automatically (Baldwin et al, 1996). Computer scoring programs are flexible and can take various sized grids (such as 8 x 8), and perform other descriptive statistics, such as the average or mean ratings, etc., for the grids being analyzed.

Summary

This chapter introduces the Personal Construct Theory of Opinion Leadership. This theory of opinion leadership explains how opinion leaders think and what they do (think multidimensionally, perceive and process large amounts of information, communicate verbally face-to-face, and effectively persuade others). It can also predict who they are (via methods described in Chapter 7).

The Personal Construct Theory of Opinion Leadership represents a major paradigm shift. With all due respect for their achievements, the new theory breaks away from the tradition established by Katz & Lazarsfeld, whose primary interest was in understanding opinion leadership at the collective or societal level. As previously noted, Katz & Lazarsfeld, and their colleagues had minimal interest in trying to understand the psychology of individual opinion leaders.

In addition, the Personal Construct Theory of Opinion Leadership introduces a new theoretical framework based on the relationship between cognitive ability, personality, and interpersonal communication.

This chapter demonstrates why cognitive complexity, a cardinal personality trait, is a major component of opinion leadership cognition and communication. The chapter also demonstrates how cognitive complexity is measured.

Action Steps

Why do you think that Allport (1961) described the *cognitive or mental structure* as the "key to the edifice of personality"? Researchers have suggested matching advertising copy to the consumers' level of cognitive complexity. What do you think about this suggestion? How would you go about doing that?

CHAPTER 3

ABSTRACT THINKING AND OPINION LEADERSHIP

Here's an interesting twist on the standard eye chart:

Figure 18: Eye Chart

Vision is important. If you don't wear glasses, you probably have close to 20-20 vision, maybe even better. The state of your eyesight is easily measured with the help of an ophthalmologist or optometrist. The idea is to see things clearly, so everything, near and far, is brought into sharp focus.

Companies usually have vision statements about their grand purpose and design, and individuals are also encouraged to have a personal vision. These statements "see" into the future, and talk about important things, such as destiny and commitment towards some desired future outcome or accomplishment. For companies, there is a need to get everyone on "the same page," so everyone is working with the same objectives in mind. For an individual, a vision statement encompasses the path and goals he or she value most. They provide a means of capturing something "visionary," allowing you to tap into your highest aspirations and desires. Because of this, vision statements are often difficult to write, for they are dealing in the realm of intangible values, and they involve abstract concepts and ideas. Often, this means we must change from concrete thinking to abstract thinking, and the concomitant use of abstract ideas and images, making them difficult to measure, articulate and grasp.

Despite this difficulty, we believe that abstract thinking is of vital importance to opinion leadership. As a variable associated with cognitive complexity, it allows the opinion leader to process complex information, and formulate messages, derived from opposing viewpoints, that communicate ideas more effectively and persuasively.

Michael Kallet (2014) has identified four components of abstract thinking ability that include:

- the ability to generalize from specific situations
- the ability to make comparisons from perceived common elements
- the ability to "connect the dots" that allows the individual to understand the relevance of events, and their consequences, and to make inferences about their impact on future issues and behavior
- the ability to understand the esoteric meaning behind words, metaphors, and images, as well as the greater or more profound meaning of events.

Abstract vs. Concrete Thinking

Let's look at how abstract thinking actually occurs. For example, if you were looking at the White House, in Washington, D.C.., what would you think about? An abstract thinker may focus on what the building symbolizes, e.g., freedom, hope, opportunity, and liberty. He may see it as a beacon to those who need to flee oppression, thereby breaking the chains of intolerance and tyranny and imprisonment. The abstract thinker may see that the White House embodies both a history and a promise of what democracy offers, regardless of one's ethnicity or religion (differencebetween.net).

Alternatively, the concrete thinker concentrates on the tangible and physical properties or attributes of material objects. The concrete thinker regards the White House as an impressive architectural structure, rather than as an esoteric symbol of freedom and deliverance (differencebetween.net).

The concrete view represents a narrower focus that restricts thinking and constrains the individual by limiting one's perception to "what the eye can see," as opposed to expanding one's consciousness to include intangible or ineffable concepts.

The abstract thinker uses analogies and metaphors to expand the thought processes into different realms of ideas, concept relationships and possibilities (Madupu & O'Cooley, 2007)

Perceiving New Realities

John Spacey (2018) suggests that abstract thinkers can devise solutions that extend beyond concrete realities. In essence, the abstract thinker creates new realities of possibility.

As an example, consider the achievement that Roger Bannister accomplished when he became the first runner to break the four-minute mile in 1954. Prior to his accomplishment, it was believed that the four-minute mile exceeded human capacity.

Bannister said that when he first realized in his mind that he could do it, he knew he could do it physically. In his book, the *Four Minute Mile,* Bannister wrote that

> "The world seemed to stand still or did not exist. The only reality was the next 200 yards of track under my feet. The tape meant finality – extinction perhaps. I felt at that moment that it was my chance to do one thing supremely well. I drove on, impelled by a combination of fear and pride."

Reality changed, at least perceptually, once Bannister crossed the finish line. The four-minute mile no longer stood as an impenetrable barrier. John Landy broke Bannister's record only seven weeks later. In the next 15 years, Bannister's impossible record was beaten over 250 times. Jim Ryan, as a senior in High School in Kansas, beat Bannister's record in 1964 and he finished 8th in that race. Since then, over 325 under-4-minute runners have won races in the last 20 years.

According to Spacey (2018), the abstract thinker has the cognitive ability to:

- Devise theories that offer new or novel conceptualizations
- Structure data into new categories of organization
- Tap into the imagination to devise novel explanations
- Design experiments to explain observations
- Use emotions to deliver information that engenders trust
- Tap into counter-factual thinking to challenge conventional answers

Abstract cognitive abilities, therefore, can lead to new insights and understandings that are, essentially, self-generated. They are not inherent in the physical characteristics of the object or situation under observation.

As a result, the abstract thinker creates a new perceptual reality or conceptualization that changes how we understand things. It is a thinking process that is adaptable and flexible, so the abstract individual can adapt their responses and reactions towards other people within one's external environment.

Abstract vs. Concrete Language

Research has also shown that abstract thinkers tend to be cognitively complex. Cognitively complex individuals use language that is also more abstract. Table 4 provides a brief comparison of some abstract vs. concrete terms:

Abstract	Concrete
Love	Holding hands
Democrat	Voter
Faith	Religion
Healthy	Muscular
Success	Company CEO

Table 4: Abstract vs. Concrete Language
(Based on Hill, 2017)

Concrete terms are associated with the five senses of sight, smell, touch, taste, and hearing. We can describe something concretely, as "the beach was hot," or abstractly, "the beach was amazing" (Hill, 2017). The concrete sentence provides one item of information about the condition of the beach. The abstract description leaves more to the imagination; it can be interpreted in myriad ways and evokes many possibilities and descriptions of what an amazing beach would be like: miles of soft sand, cool blue ocean, rows of lush palm trees and beautiful resorts, kids laughing in the surf, well-tanned bathers, etc. (Anguilla-beaches.com). The abstract description provides a great deal more information.

Abstract thinkers use abstract language terms, while concrete individuals use concrete descriptions. In contrast to concrete thinkers, abstract individuals would have access to a greater range of information, including multiple meanings and subtle nuances that may exist.

Abstract Thinking and Communication

In addition, abstract thinkers discern more information about the individuals with whom they are communicating, and they can adapt information via messages that will stand a greater chance of resonating with their listeners, thereby making their arguments more acceptable and persuasive.

Using abstract concepts, therefore, improves the individual's communication efforts by increasing their ability to verbalize messages. Such messages can be conveyed more effectively due to the abstract thinker's enhanced understanding of other people and their viewpoints (Delia, Clark & Switzer, 1974).

Abstract thinking has also been found to be associated with the thinking processes of cognitively complex individuals, and with their ability to communicate effectively and persuasively with other individuals. It provides the ability to generate a deep understanding of a topic of interest, and an ability to articulate that information in persuasive and compelling ways.

The Personal Construct Theory of Opinion Leadership, therefore, views abstract thinking as an integral personality trait that is an indispensable characteristic of opinion leadership.

Summary

This chapter describes how the opinion leader thinks abstractly, and the advantages it provides compared to a concrete thinker.

Abstract thinking gives the individual a greater amount and range of information. It allows for the use of metaphors and analogies which can provide new insights that factual information can't address.

Abstract thinking allows one to see things creatively in novel ways and to imagine new possibilities and relationships among objects or topics. By thinking abstractly, new realities are formed. Roger Bannister is a case in point; after he realized that he could break the four-minute mile, the physical obstacle no longer mattered.

Abstract thinkers tend to use abstract language that expands their thought processes and results. They grasp new insights and understanding of phenomena. Often, they obtain new information that is self-generated, and that is, therefore, not limited by the five senses.

Invariably, the abstract thinker understands more about their immediate environment. They can feel confident and use self-disclosure, without fear, in order to establish rapport with others.

Most importantly, they understand other people to a greater extent than individuals who think concretely, and they have an innate sense of what the other person needs or is thinking about. In this way, the abstract person can craft a custom-made message based on their perception and discernment of others. These messages are effective and persuasive.

Action Steps

Look at the following painting, Renoir's *Woman with a Cat*, painted in 1875.

Figure 19: Renoir's Woman with a Cat
Pierre-Auguste Renoir, 1841-1919

First, let's look at it from a very concrete perspective, just using the five physical senses. What do you see? Using concrete or physical terms, how would you describe what you see to someone else?

Now, using abstract terms, how would you describe the painting and what you see or experience?

How do the two descriptions differ? Can you explain why an opinion leader would use abstract terms?

CHAPTER 4

AMBIGUITY TOLERANCE AND OPINION LEADERSHIP

Consider the following traffic signs and determine when (or even if) you can legally park your car there?

Figure 20: Confusing Traffic Signs

Humans are constantly inundated with confusing and contradictory information. Sometimes we struggle to make sense of what we consciously see or hear (such as in the traffic signs shown above). Often, however, our internal cognitive processes are challenged to resolve internal conflicts caused by contradictory information or confusing directions that we encounter.

Some people have a high tolerance for ambiguity. For example, they can be exposed to confusing information, and yet they can assimilate several opposing viewpoints with little mental or emotional stress. For others, their tolerance for any inconsistency or ambiguity is very limited. The latter individuals simply cannot entertain contradictory information. Like cognitively simple individuals, they view things as either black or white, or "yes" or "no," with no room for "maybe" allowed.

Integrating Opposing viewpoints

Ambiguity Tolerance (AT) enables individuals to process information, and to select messages carefully in a way that is compatible with listener needs or viewpoints. The information may be unpleasant or disagreeable for some, but the ambiguity tolerant person can decipher ambiguity, which allows them to understand an alternative or contrary point of view.

According to Furnham & Marks (2013), for those scoring high on ambiguity tolerance, "ambiguous situations are perceived as desirable, challenging and interesting."

Ambiguity tolerance, therefore, describes a mental structure in which the individual can integrate opposing viewpoints with little or no internal difficulty or stress. In contrast, for individuals who are low in ambiguity tolerance, the reaction is quite different.

According to Furnham & Marks (2013):

> "Generally, for those with low TA, there is an aversive reaction to ambiguous situations because the lack of information makes it difficult to assess risk and correctly make a decision. These situations are perceived as a threat and source of discomfort. Reactions to the perceived threat are stress, avoidance, delay, suppression, or denial" (Furnham et al, 2013).

An individual with low ambiguity tolerance may experience significant stress and discomfort when faced with a situation that is confusing or contradictory.

The individual 's inability to tolerate ambiguity is viewed by Frenkel-Brunswik (1949) as

> "a tendency to resort to black-and-white solutions, to arrive at premature closure as to evaluative aspects, often at the neglect of reality, and to seek for unqualified and unambiguous overall acceptance and rejection of other people."

The ambiguity intolerant personality appears more prejudgmental, and reflects a preference for concrete, unequivocal types of information.

In psychology, ambiguity tolerance is treated as a personality trait which pertains to how the individual reacts emotionally and perceptually to ambiguous stimuli (Norton, 1975; Frenkel-Brunswik, 1949).

Ambiguity Tolerance and Cognitive Complexity

It's been reported that cognitively complex individuals have considerable ability to integrate heterogeneous or conflicting stimulus information. Cognitively complex individuals appear to form multivariate impressions of phenomena (that is, perceiving multiple outcomes or elements simultaneously) by combining or integrating both positive and negative attributes. Such integrated impressions of phenomena appear to be formed more quickly than impressions by less complex individuals (Delia et al, 1974).

Tripodi & Bieri (1966) suggest that cognitively complex individuals may also have a structural preference for multidimensional information sources or topics (e.g., things having different parts of features). Cognitively simple people appear to prefer highly organized, unequivocal environments, where simple observation may be used to understand stimuli behaviors and attributes. Thus, the cognitively complex individual can cope with ambiguous or confusing information. They not only process more information, but they do so more effectively than less complex individuals.

These observations suggest that cognitively complex individuals tend to tolerate stimuli inconsistencies. Cognitively simple individuals reject ambiguous or discordant information to defend their positions and egos. In contrast, cognitively complex individuals form ideas that incorporate new information, whether or not they agree with it. In addition, they do not impulsively reject or discount adverse information, so new facts and viewpoints are more easily assimilated by them (Muneno & Dembo, 1982).

Ambiguity tolerance is also related to how the cognitively complex person engages other people (Parker, 1972). By considering and evaluating opposing viewpoints, they are able to form persuasive counterarguments. The ambiguity tolerant individual appears less defensive and more willing to consider the efficacy of opposing views. Such behavior may help to ingratiate the individual with others during group discussions.

Ambiguity Tolerance and Opinion Leadership

The relationship of ambiguity tolerance to one's effectiveness in group discussions is also relevant to the role of ambiguity tolerance and opinion leadership. Consider the opinion leader in a marketing context, for example. Since the opinion leader engages in interpersonal communication about products and service purchases, the existence of ambiguity tolerance would assist the opinion leader in understanding and persuading those consumers who appear to be reluctant, non-adopters of new products or technology. With a high level of ambiguity tolerance, the opinion leader has a greater ability to consider the reasons for non-adoption, such as perceived risk, which can then be addressed to assuage the listener's apprehension and uncertainty.

The opinion leader attends to the other person's needs and reasons involving the adoption or non-adoption of products. Thus, the opinion leader can cope with ambiguous or confusing information. They are not only able to process conflicting information, but they also integrate and use that information persuasively.

Tolerance for ambiguity has been called a "gateway to leadership opportunity" (Mathias-Sager, 2018). Researchers have found that the ability to withstand uncertainty and change also supports a number of qualities associated with leadership style and decision-making, including mindfulness, flexibility, risk-taking, creativity and innovation, entrepreneurship and managerial performance (Brendel et al, 2016).

Summary

Ambiguity tolerance has been called the "gateway to leadership opportunity." It reflects a flexible and adaptable mental structure by which individuals can deal with new or ambiguous stimuli and internalize disparate viewpoints without stress.

They can tailor-make messages using conflicting information and appeal to others by extracting arguments that fit the current audience and situation.

The ambiguity tolerant person is not hampered by indecision or uncertainty. They look for creative or mindful solutions to make progress. They are not hampered if they don't understand everything, and they show resilience by persevering with limited or imperfect information.

Ambiguity intolerant individuals tend to be judgmental and dogmatic, and they find it difficult to resolve things that lack continuity or lie somewhere in-between opposing arguments. It is difficult for ambiguity intolerant individuals to change their views and compromise. They may show indecisiveness, or else rush to some premature judgement. Since ambiguous situations involve risk and uncertainty, which are emotionally disturbing, the ambiguity intolerant goal is to limit ambiguity caused by the lack of a clear-cut solution.

Ambiguity tolerance is closely aligned with cognitive complexity. It allows the individual to comprehend the existence of opposing or conflicting viewpoints, and to consider the motivations and actions of different individuals so that the opinion leader can achieve a closer rapport while talking about topics of mutual interest.

Action Steps

A store is trying to sell a new, innovative toaster oven that uses infrared heat which cooks from the inside out. Two customers are looking at the new toaster oven; one customer is ambiguity tolerant while the other is ambiguity intolerant.

When talking about the product, how should the salesperson adapt the description of the product to the two potential buyers? Which one would be more likely to buy?

CHAPTER 5

EMPATHY AND OPINION LEADERSHIP

*"Could a greater miracle take place than for us to look
through each other's eyes for an instant?"*
–Henry David Thoreau

Michele Borba, Ph.D., coined a great term, "**Un**selfie," as the title of her book about recognizing the need to empower kids who show empathetic tendencies but who grow up in "our all-about-me world" (Borba, 2017). We seem to be surrounded by a society that values self-image and self-centeredness above all else. In contrast, empathy reflects a personality characteristic that is all about developing a deeper rapport or understanding of other people, as well as reaching out and connecting with them.

As Siebert (1996) defines it, empathy is "the ability to absorb what another person thinks or feels." It also increases our understanding of our immediate environment, which also gives us an ability to perceive reality more accurately.

Empathy And "I-Thou"

The need to bridge the interpersonal gulf is, perhaps, best expressed by the "I-Thou" philosophy of Martin Buber (Kramer, 2012). As a means of ending conflict, Buber believed in the importance of interpersonal communication and the necessity of dialogue based on how we see and treat others.

As Buber has said,

> "in a genuine dialogue each of the partners, even when he stands in opposition to the other, heeds, affirms, and confirms his opponent as an existing other" (Friedman, 2012).

Buber saw that people can approach the world from a perspective of self-absorption, using an "I-It" perspective, in which the I is limited to oneself and the world is limited to egoistic sensations about impersonal "it" things. When personal perception is outwardly transformed, the I-Thou perspective can then establish a world based on relationships, participation, and intimacy (Popova, 2018).

Getting to the "I-Thou" state, where you address the other as thou (and not "it"), requires a change in which one's ego is no longer the center of its own universe. The emphasis of the individual changes to a focus on the "meeting" or relationship you establish with another person. Intimacy, acknowledging and caring about the other person, becomes the cornerstone or focal point of reality and living.

Stepping Outside One's Self

In reviewing Buber's philosophy, Maria Popova suggests that "one must step outside one's self. Only then does the Other cease to be a means to one's own ends and becomes real" (Popova, 2018). A new reality is thus created when a genuine relationship and meeting between two or more individuals occurs.

The need to put aside the ego is also characteristic of Morita psychotherapy, a therapeutic system developed in Japan by Shoma Morita. The conditions being treated are called "shinkeishitsu," illness or anxiety caused by problems with other people. The treatment redirects the patient from an almost complete inner fixation or obsession with their own thoughts, towards becoming outwardly engaged in activities with other people (Morita et al, 1998, Reynolds, 1976).

In Frans De Waal's (2009) book, *The Age of Empathy*, he describes our cultural dilemma as, "we walk on two legs: a social leg and a selfish leg." The key to living as an effective human is to understand how to balance appropriately between those two forces. De Waal implies that it is primarily the fear of social consequences that impel people to act empathetically and to assist other people when needed. He also suggests that empathy is aroused generally for those who are close to us and for whom we care the most, such as our family, friends, and associates in our network.

The role of opinion leader may also be engendered by an interest in other people, rather than as a selfish concern for enhancing one's social status, a means of increasing one's reputation, or some sort of product or shopping compulsion.

Pattern Empathy

Al Siebert (1996) describes pattern empathy as the ability to understand the interconnections of things during events and the prediction of how those events will turn out. What he means is that the empathetic individual can understand the pattern of social interactions that occur within groups, including cause and effect relationships. The empathetic individual learns by observing and assessing the nature of the contacts among group members and predicting how different individuals will interact with each other.

Siebert (1996) suggests that the ability to construe context as things unfold is shared among people who are intimately involved in leading an event with others, such as performers, athletes, educators, military officers, and musicians, among others. Within this group dynamic, he lists "group leaders." The inclusion of group leaders no doubt includes opinion leaders, who interpret cues from the environment to guide their own, and the group's, actions and responses.

Pattern empathy gives the opinion leader "street smarts," an ability to keep in tune with group members so that he or she can effectively lead group discussions and/or decision situations. Using pattern empathy, the opinion leader can immediately sense what others may be thinking or feeling and how to respond appropriately to their concerns.

Empathy and Communication

The concept of empathy suggests that some people have a greater sensitivity and ability to understand other people. This has been viewed by some as the capacity for "insight into the temporary moods or underlying personality traits of others" (Chlopan et al, 1985).

Some people appear to have

> "the ability to respond intuitively and empathetically to others and to group situations. A person high on this variable would be described as insightful, perceptive and discerning, as having the knack of "sizing up" social situations and of making sound and dependable evaluations of people. He will respond to nuances and subtleties of behavior which might escape the notice of others and will possess a flair for interpreting his observations" (Hogan 1969).

In viewing empathy as an exchange process, Hogan (1969) found that highly empathetic subjects communicated more effectively in social situations (e.g., communicated ideas more completely). Highly empathetic people also appear to perceive their surroundings more accurately than do those with lower empathy levels. Higher levels of empathy also appear related to higher levels of emotional arousal in social situations and to an interest in helping others.

The difference in empathy levels of cognitively complex and cognitively simple individuals has also been characterized as a progression from being ego-oriented to being other-oriented. The orientation of cognitively complex individuals is towards a disposition to understand others (by making inferences about the underlying motivational and situational states of others), as opposed to being prejudgmental or evaluatively disposed (Alvy, 1971; Hale & Delia, 1976).

A high level of empathy has been noted as a key element in effective interpersonal communication (Hale, 1980). Cognitively complex individuals evidently adapt their communication strategies based on empathy or social perspective-taking, e.g., the degree to which they base their communications on perceptions of listener needs and characteristics.

Some researchers advise that

> "making communications-relevant inferences about listener characteristics is a prerequisite to formulating listener-adapted communications' (Delia & Clark, 1977).

A Listener Adapted Orientation

According to Zajonc (1960), this listener adapted orientation relates to the speaker's anticipation of inducing change in the listener's cognitive structure. Zajonc (1960) notes that although speakers ordinarily reflect greater structural unity and organization, presumably in pursuit of their purpose, individuals who are frequent communicators also show a higher level of differentiation (e.g., are cognitively complex) compared to individuals who end up as listeners (and are cognitively simple). The communicator's higher level of differentiation suggests the use of multiple dimensions and the capacity to consider the listener's perspectives.

The empathy literature and the cognitive complexity literature together suggest that empathy is an essential part of effective interpersonal communication. By reflecting an empathetic interest and concern for others, the cognitively complex individual may secure a persuasive or leadership role by gaining the listener confidence and trust.

The interpersonal skills of the empathetic individual appear to relate to the informal communication role of the opinion leader. High empathy levels seem likely to be related to the opinion leader's ability to exchange new product opinions and information in a listener-oriented, persuasive manner. Thus, the existence of empathy would be theorized to be part of the personality configuration associated with opinion leadership.

The empathetic qualities of the communicator should also be enhanced by the overall communication manner exhibited by the speaker, including the types and range of expression and cues used. To establish rapport and understanding with others, the emotional communicator must able to convey a range of emotion and concern.

Since an ability to adapt verbal messages has been associated with cognitive complexity, the next chapter considers an individual's ability to utilize different communications styles, and non-verbal elements of communication, and their importance to opinion leadership.

Summary

Being empathetic is important for sales, for management, for having effective relationships, and for being an opinion leader. It's all about letting people know you care!

Empathy includes the ability to understand how other people think and feel. As an exchange process, it enhances one's efforts to communicate more effectively in social situations. Highly empathetic individuals are in tune with other people, and this helps them to understand their surroundings more quickly and accurately than other individuals.

To be empathetic, one needs to put aside one's ego and to view others as individuals rather than as objects. This is the basic idea espoused in Martin Buber's "I-Thou" model of communication.

Similarly, Morita psychotherapy in Japan emphasizes the need to adopt an outward orientation towards others that prevents one from being overly self-absorbed. For opinion leadership, this means acting as a "social being" and having a genuine interest in other people.

It also means having certain "street smarts" – observing and understanding social situations and predicting how others will act. This involves gaining an insight into other people and responding appropriately.

Empathy also means acting as a listener-adapted communicator – anticipating one's impact on other people, and understanding how to induce change in other people's attitudes and behavior. To do so, one must be able to employ different communication styles as situations unfold and change.

Action Steps

Let's practice being empathetic!

The next time you are buying something in a store -- even if it's just for a moment while purchasing coffee at a local shop – ask the store salesperson something personal: "how do you put up with the stress of having to serve so many people each morning" or "how do you stay on your feet for so many hours," or compliment them on something, "that's a great tattoo, what does it mean?" or "I love that ring, where did you get it?" (By the way, I did this once at the Motor Vehicle Dept window, and the female clerk actually handed me her diamond engagement ring to look at!). It can be a quick conversation. Hopefully, you can connect authentically and get a real response.

What were your results of this brief excursion into empathy? What does it suggest about your future interactions with people in general?

CHAPTER 6

LEADERSHIP ORIENTATION, EXPRESSIVENESS & CHARISMA

"Charisma is the intangible that makes people want to follow you, to be around you, to be influenced by you."
–Roger Dawson

The characteristics in this chapter - leadership orientation, expressiveness, and charisma - are closely linked with the concept of opinion leadership. They also help explain the way in which communication occurs among opinion leaders and followers.

The Importance of Leadership Ability

History suggests that leadership can often determine success or failure in highly critical situations. During the Civil War, Abraham Lincoln was concerned about officers who, in his view, failed to take pre-emptive action, thereby missing chances to defeat the enemy. In effect, Lincoln questioned their leadership ability.

He was particularly frustrated by Major General John C. Fremont's disorganized command, as well as Fremont's recurring failure to attack opposing troops, despite Lincoln's orders to take immediate action against Confederate forces.

On April 9, 1861, Lincoln relieved Freemont of command, noting that

> "his cardinal mistake is that he isolates himself and allows nobody to see him; by which he does not know what is going on in the very matter he is dealing with" (Phillips, 1993).

Lincoln offered the following advice to his command about how they should conduct themselves with others (Phillips, 1993). Part of that advice emphasizes the value of information. In some ways, these remarks represent Lincoln's own guide on becoming an opinion leader, e.g., a source and disseminator of information:

- You must seek, and require access to, reliable and up-to-date information
- It is important that the people know you come among them
- Don't often decline to see people who call on you
- Be the very embodiment of good temper and affability
- Offer advice on how to solve problems
- Remember, everyone like a compliment

Lincoln appears to suggest that leadership competency can be learned.

A similar assessment of leadership puts It this way:

> "Leadership is applicable to all facets of life: a competency that you can learn to expand your perspective, set the context of a goal, understand the dynamics of human behavior and take the initiative to get to where you want to be" (www.coachtree.com).

According to Yukl (1989), leadership involves influence. He advises that leaders are essential for

"Influencing task objectives and strategies, influencing commitment and compliance in task behavior to achieve those objectives, influencing group maintenance and identification, and influencing the culture of an organization."

Influence is also the raison d'être of opinion leadership. The Personal Construct Theory of Opinion Leadership suggests that the opinion leader can influence others by virtue of possessing key personality characteristics associated with persuasive communication.

Although a leadership orientation implies that the individual possesses the ability and inclination to act as a leader, this does not mean that the individual dominates nor monopolizes conversations with others. It suggests that opinion leadership can become manifest under different circumstances, e.g., when a discussion turns to a topic of interest; when other personalities are seeking advice or recommendations; and when no one else competes for control or tries to monopolize the conversation.

As Katz and Lazarsfeld (1955) indicated, opinion leadership is exercised indirectly and discretely. Often, non-leaders may spontaneously turn to the opinion leader, often in response to suggestions or ideas that the opinion leader has expressed. The opinion leader may become the central figure within a network, evidencing many requests for information from others within the group.

The task-oriented vs relationship-oriented dichotomy provides a classic way of looking at one's leadership orientation. The task-oriented leader, for example, is committed to achieving performance goals above all else. In this view, efficiency and deadlines are paramount. People are viewed as resources who are expendable (Bean-Mellinger, 2019). Management who callously feel this way often engage in downsizing full-time employees in favor of outsourcing whenever possible.

In contrast, the relationship-oriented leader recognizes that tasks must be carried out successfully through people. This leadership orientation is concerned with individual welfare and making sure that people engage in tasks that are meaningful and satisfactory. In the realm of opinion leadership, this means showing an interest in others by helping them understand their choices in order to make optimal decisions (Bean-Mellinger, 2019).

Another helpful approach, for understanding how the concept leadership applies to opinion leadership, is to consider the difference between a manager and a leader. Although the terms are often used interchangeably, it's been suggested that "the essential difference appears to be that leaders influence commitment, whereas managers merely carry out position responsibilities" (Yutl, 1989). Since opinion leaders have no hierarchical authority, it is essential that they interact effectively with their followers.

A similar approach is found in the idea of "principle-centered leadership," advocated by Covey & Gulledge (1992), in which they stress core, "people-based," determinants of effective leadership: internalizing a culture of quality, and total integrity. According to the authors, "we perfect relationships by making and receiving deposits to emotional bank accounts – by building trust." Although their advice is geared to an organizational context, much of what the authors say applies equally well to individual relationships.

Thus, they state,

> "It is not strategy but identity, the core of unchanging principles and commitment to shared vision and mission, which enables the constancy of purpose necessary for long-term success."

For opinion leaders, the identity reflects their overall character, and how authentic and genuine they appear to be in making recommendations that followers will value. Whether they are followed or not depends on how they are perceived and evaluated.

Their demeanor and behavior include a host of ways in which the opinion leader communicates to the followers. Accordingly, we now turn to components of that process.

Expressiveness

Expressiveness, or affective communication, is most often defined as an ability to convey emotion, not only verbally, but nonverbally. Leadership orientation allows one to communicate persuasively and effectively with others, often in ways that go beyond simple, verbal expression.

With interpersonal communication, researchers have indicated that words account for only about 10% of the meaning conveyed; vocal tone about 35%; and non-verbal communication, 55% (Steiner, 2018). Thus, vocal tone, facial expression, body language, gestures and so forth, are exceedingly important.

Non-verbal communication also includes silence. As General Charles DeGaulle (1960) once said, "rien ne rehausese l'autorite, mieux que le silence" – "*nothing enhances authority better than silence.*" It takes but a frown, a pause, a look, and disapproval is communicated instantly. Silence is a potent source of meaning.

The ability to communicate non-verbally (or silently) is similarly captured in Robert Benchley's somewhat cryptic remark, "drawing on my fine command of the English language, I said nothing." Sometimes our most effective communications occur silently, without the use of language or words.

I recently saw a photo about the Holocaust posted on Facebook, accompanied by the caption, "NO WORDS NEEDED." It was an extremely eloquent post.

Expressive people have been described as being capable of using a range of verbal and nonverbal "cues to move, lead, inspire, or captivate others" (Friedman et al, 1980). According to the authors, the ability to communicate a range of expression and emotion involves the individual's ability to persuade others and is thus part of social interaction.

Aside from verbal content, there are implicit communication patterns we frequently use, but which we rarely recognize consciously. John Gottman (2018), for example, has developed a system that analyzes interpersonal "bids" which can be a "question, a gesture, a look, a touch" – any expression that says, "I want to feel connected to you." Responses to a "bid" may range from being positive (in which the participants engage in supportive communication and actions) to being negative (in which a response imbues anger, attack or confrontation), or indifference (in which no real connection exists). Positive bids reflect relationships that tend to survive, while indifferent and negative exchanges mark communication and relationship failure.

Friedman et al (1980) report finding expressive communication patterns in activities such as lecturing behavior, political activity, theatrical experience, personal selling, and social influence and interaction.

Opinion leaders, who are active social communicators, also reflect significant levels of expressive ability. Expressiveness provides additional insight into the verbal and non-verbal range of communication skills associated with opinion leadership.

Charisma

Historically, charisma has been viewed as an intangible quality, a type of enigmatic "personal magnetism" that enables an individual to attract and influence others.

In recent years, the concept of charisma has been refined into a more formal and logical "neo-charismatic theory of leadership," with a scientific emphasis on its emotional component. The focus now is on the leader's ability to express emotions which can create an intense emotional link between the leader and his/her followers (Bono & Ilies, 2016; House & Aditya, 1997). Charisma can be defined as an "emotional attachment to the leader" (Bono & Ilies, 2016). The researchers suggest a model of emotional interaction as shown below:

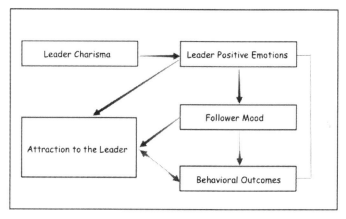

Figure 21: Leader Charisma: Use of Positive Emotions
(Adapted from Bono & Ilies, 2016)

Bono & Ilies (2016) suggest that the positive emotions expressed by charismatic leaders create positive moods in their followers. This emotional transference is the cement that bonds leader and followers together.

Charismatic leadership also involves the use of language. The ability to convey emotion verbally creates a strong bond with followers. In extreme cases, the charismatic leader may absolve followers of personal risks and decision-making responsibility.

The Survivor Personality

Earlier in this book, in Figure 8, on page 44, we listed various labels that researchers have used to describe opinion leaders (or others who disseminate information). Perhaps you noticed that the term, "survivors," appeared on the bottom of that list. We suggest that survivors and opinion leaders may share several commonalities.

In his book, *The Survivor Personality*, Al Siebert (1996) suggests that survivors actively try to understand and interpret external situations in order to devise appropriate responses (either verbally or physically). Above all else, survivors also cultivate *positive attitudes* which give them confidence and resilience to deal with people and changing situations.

Table 5: Importance of Positive Attitudes/ Follower Mood (adapted from Siebert, 1996)

In addition to creating a positive mood, these survivor characteristics are strikingly similar to the mental and verbal agility often used to describe cognitively complex individuals.

As described by Siebert (1996), these traits include adaptability, conscious awareness, inner-guidedness, intuitiveness, inquisitiveness, and active learning. These dimensions would seem to provide individuals with a considerable amount of cognitive and emotional versatility, adaptability and strength of character.

The "MacGyver-like" tendencies that survivors use to assess situations and react to those around them in meaningful and persuasive ways, appear applicable to the current discussion. For opinion leaders, this would mean having the ability to adapt more effectively to different types of audiences and information seekers. Thus, the survivor personality trait pattern may be a fruitful area for further opinion leadership related study.

The Johari Window

Another possible way of looking at opinion leader/follower interactions is by using a model that focuses on social exchanges, called the Johari Window. The model was developed in 1955 by psychologists, Joseph Luft, and Harrington Ingram, and has been used in organizational settings to improve communication among *leaders and groups*. This approach offers a dynamic view of the cognitive and interpersonal communications processes that occur among individuals.

Surprisingly, a board game called *KnowMe*, based on the Johari Window, was developed in 1994 by Matthews Bullen and Associates. Its purpose also was to help participants learn about interpersonal communication and thus facilitate dialogues within groups. The Johari Window has been used to help leaders determine how to deal with individuals in groups who hold dissimilar ideas or opinions (Gaw, 1976; Holmes, 2000).

Opinion Leadership research could potentially employ the Johari model to provide additional insight into the opinion leadership communication process, including understanding how messages and information are adapted to different participants (such as friends, strangers, family members, etc.) and to different personality types (e.g., people who are open-minded versus people who are hidden or secretive, etc.).

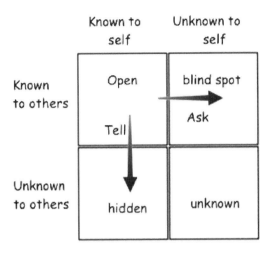

Figure 22: The Johari Window

Summary

In this chapter, we discussed the relationship of opinion leadership with several traits: leadership orientation, expressiveness, and charisma.

Leadership orientation involves interactions that influence the behavior of other people. In order to be effective, the leadership-oriented individual needs to be relationship or people oriented. One way to do this is by using an array of communication styles.

Expressive opinion leaders, for example, can convey emotion. They also communicate via non-verbal elements – body language, gestures, etc. With a large array of expressive techniques, they can communicate more effectively and persuasively.

Opinion leaders may also evidence charismatic traits. Charisma is considered to be related to leadership qualities, rather than some mysterious, invisible force. To a large extent, the charismatic leader uses language in a manner that establishes a strong, emotional bond with followers.

Surprisingly, opinion leaders also appear to share traits associated with the survivor personality, including ingenuity, creativeness, adaptability, and intuitiveness. These characteristics may allow an individual to assess situations very quickly in order to adapt to new circumstances and formulate appropriate responses to conditions or to nearby individuals.

The Johari Window also seems to be a practical framework for assessing difficult situations that the opinion leader could face. Developed by two psychologists, the Johari Window is used to help people learn how to communicate with adverse personality types, particularly with individuals who may be negative, obstinate or secretive.

Action Steps

Is there someone you know who is charismatic? How would you describe that person and their interactions with other people? Do you feel that charisma is an inherited personality trait or something that can be learned?

Ask the person about their charisma, particularly to see if they are aware of it and if they had a parent or grandparent who exhibited the same personality characteristics. What did you learn?

CHAPTER 7

WHO ARE THE OPINION LEADERS?

Vince Lisi

Figure 23: Spiritual Teacher

Vince is a man with a special calling. Vince teaches weekly spiritual study groups that meet in Ohio, Indiana, and Pennsylvania. One of his groups meets weekly on skype. Vince also serves as a chaplain in the spiritual care department of St. Elizabeth Hospital Medical Center.

Vince founded Now Creations, an online site where people can sign up for his study groups which explore contemporary books of spiritual teachings, including *A Course in Miracles, Life & Teachings of the Masters of the Far East, Oneness* by Rasha, and *A Course in Mastering Alchemy* by Jim Self.

With his usual Namaste greeting, Vince teaches us to see the divinity and goodness in all beings and creatures on earth. Vince is a good and noble soul who feels that the world is experiencing an amazing growth in spiritual consciousness that will help bring peace to humanity.

Jim Morrison

Figure 24: Master of Mechanical Advantage

When Jim moved from Arizona to South Carolina, I'm sure that his former neighbors felt a profound sense of loss and angst. When his neighbors needed help with fixing just about anything – car repair, electrical wiring, carpentry, plumbing, sod installation, you name it – Jim was eager to help and did so enthusiastically and cheerfully.

As an FAA certified aircraft maintenance technician, Jim has spent much of his 30-year working career as a Supervisor of aircraft maintenance technicians, at UPS and at American West airlines before that. He made sure that each $200 million 747 jet flew as expected, with no mechanical problems.

People invariably turn to Jim for product and vendor advice. For example, when Jim had several PODS delivered with his belongings from Arizona, one neighbor (who was looking to rent some PODS himself), sought Jim's endorsement of the firm he had chosen. Similarly, when Jim had new windows and French doors installed recently, the installer's name and contact information were soon sought after.

During the aftermath of Hurricane Matthew, Jim hired a crane company to remove several tons of trees that had been felled by the storm. Other neighbors soon did the same. When anything needs fixing, Jim is the "oracle" his neighbors consult first.

Edward Like

Figure 25: Community Leader

If we gave Ed Like a title, it would no doubt be the unofficial Mayor of Dataw Island, South Carolina! Ed understands the pulse and rhythm of his island home, and he's always up to date as to current events, Country Club news, and people moving in or out.

Ed has an incredible talent for cultivating people. Ed is the founder of the Dataw Defense and Lunch League, a group of some 50 or so gun enthusiasts (aka "old guys with guns") who go to target practice on Thursdays each week. Ed also founded and coordinates the Boys Night Out Movie Group, now 30 strong, which gathers for dinner and a movie each Tuesday night.

At 81, Ed is also a man of enormous energy. He is well known as the President of the Board of the Beaufort Symphony Orchestra. With a mischievous glint in his eye, Ed usually jokes that he's in his 12th year of a two-year term. Keeping a symphony orchestra running and solvent in a town of thirteen thousand people isn't easy, which is why no one else has volunteered to take the job!

105

Ed convinces local businesses and donors to renew their support for the Symphony each year. Always smiling and energetic, how can anyone say no to this veritable force of nature?

Harry Shapiro

Figure 26: Creative Connoisseur

Harry Shapiro is a charismatic tour-de-force. He always makes everyone feel special and important. Low key, amiable, and always inquisitive, Harry loves fine wines, and he keeps his wine collection in what he calls, his "wine basement," avoiding the more pretentious term, "wine cellar." That sense of understatement is one of Harry's most endearing qualities. And, when Harry suggests a wine, you can be sure it will be a good one!

Harry recalls that he learned one of his most important lessons from his father: "enjoy the finer things in life, but always be happy with what you have." His home is impeccably furnished with meaningful artwork (many by his wife, Ilene), and fixtures hand-picked by Harry himself. Harry finds the best of what's available, and he's happy to help others make better choices too.

Harry is the retired creative VP of Signet Inc., where he developed creative ads for Kay Jewelers and other brands, showing his deep connection to the feelings and emotional chords of his audience.

Harry's wife, Ilene, tells the story of when they went to Europe and were part of a bicycle group of tourists. When the group split into two factions, both groups claimed Harry as theirs.

Observations About These "Ordinary" Opinion Leaders

We can make some observations about the people we have identified above as opinion leaders:

1) In each case, their personalities draw them to people (and people to them).
2) They are virtually surrounded by people whom they have cultivated.
3) Their interest in people appears genuine and not only for personal gain.
4) They are fully engaged with people on a regular basis.
5) In addition to engaging in product related conversations with others, some opinion leaders provide non-verbal cues as well by buying products that others see and emulate. Thus, they may legitimize product and brand choices, and pave the way for others to make similar acquisitions.
6) Opinion leaders also express their helpfulness and connection to people through their job-related expertise.

In the next section, we move to identifying opinion leaders using several methods, including a process measure which can also validate the Personal Construct model and its ability to find opinion leaders who might not be apparent by other means.

Let's start with a transcript of a recording of a small group of six individuals engaged in a conversation about bank services. The transcript identifies each of their comments as to whom it is "From" and the person "To" whom it was directed. Note that #7 is the group as a whole, which is included since some comments may be directed at all of the members rather than one or two.

A Process Measure of Opinion Leadership

Let's eavesdrop on a group of six consumers discussing the use of an ATM. The comments were recorded and are tallied below:

From	To:	Comment
#3	#6	I prefer to bank with a teller
#6	#3	Really? I like using the ATM
#3	#2	I find the ATM very convenient
#2	#3	I've used the ATM, but I often forget my password
#3	#4	By the way, I think we should rebel against bank charges for using another bank's ATM
#4	#3	I hadn't noticed that since I stick with my bank's ATM's
#6	#3	Mine doesn't charge for that
#1	#7	I find that ATM's aren't that convenient
#3	#4	I hate waiting in line in the bank. On a Friday, a lot of people are still making deposits or cashing checks, and I don't want to be behind 10 people
#4	#3	I've never had to wait in line
#5	#3	You have to have your card, but at another bank you may not get the highest amount back

Figure 27: Group Discussion of Banking Service

When looking at the tally of comments made by each group member, we look to see which group member generated and received the greatest number of comments. We would classify that individual as an opinion leader. According to Table 6, you can see immediately that member #3 is the opinion leader for this group.

Group Member	From	To	Total
1	1	0	1
2	1	1	2
3	4	6	10
4	2	2	4
5	1	0	1
6	2	1	3
7*	0	1	1
Total	11	11	22

(#7* is the group as a whole)
Table 6: Tally of Participant Comments

As defined previously, opinion leaders engage in face-to-face, interpersonal communication. To assess the efficacy of an observational measure, we recorded 52 groups talking about the use or purchase of products or services. We predicted that the cognitively complex individuals would emerge as the opinion leaders who initiated and received the most comments in their respective groups. A content analysis of those conversations indicated the frequency and direction of comments.

The Bales, Strodtbeck, Mills, and Rosenborough (1951) Interaction Matrix technique was used to determine opinion leader identities. The utility of this method is that it assesses the rank order of group members according to originating and targeted comments (including comments directed to the group), and total comments. The number of comments which each person generated and received is entered into the matrix. These totals can then be rank ordered, thereby reflecting the relative amount of participation of each group member.

According to Bales, Strodtbeck, Mils, and Rosenborough (1951), the top-ranked speaker "is acting as a kind of communications center, and in this sense is performing a leadership function."

In applying this method to opinion leadership, the individual who initiated and received the greatest number of comments was designated as the opinion leader; the individual with the least number of initiated and received comments was the non-leader.

It should be noted that the total number of comments, which constitutes the process measure of opinion leadership, differs according to group size. To compensate for group size differences (e.g. some groups might have 3-4 members, others 5-6 members and so forth), it's important to determine the rank order of comments within the discussion group.

Group "A"		Group "B"	
# Comments	Rank Order	# Comments	Rank Order
63	1	156	1
53	2	120	2
19	3	105	3
10	4	90	4
5	5	83	5
		74	6
		63	7

Table 7: Importance of Rank Ordering Comments

The identification of opinion leaders by total comments in their respective groups can be determined after a rank ordering of group members is made in order to compare the subjects across groups (Bales, Strodtbeck, Mills & Rosenborough, 1951; Bales, 1970; Brilhart, 1988). A rank ordering is analogous to standardizing differently scaled measures so comparisons may be made across groups (Dillon, Madden & Firtle, 2004). To illustrate, Table 7 lists the rankings for two different sized groups that discussed the same topic.

According to the rank order of comments, the subject with 63 comments in group A is the opinion leader, while the subject with 63 comments in group B is an opinion follower. A comparison of the absolute measures of total comments would be meaningless. The use of a group design similarly affects comparisons of other variables as well, necessitating the use of rank order techniques for group comparisons and data analysis.

Interrater Reliability

In order to determine the total number of comments initiated and received (e.g., frequency and direction of comments), for each subject, it's important to have several individuals independently and objectively code the videotaped group discussions.

Pearson product-moment correlations can be used to compute reliability by using the number of comments determined by each rater for the group members (which constitutes "ratio" data). In a sample of comments from 5 groups, the correlation for the number of comments initiated by the subjects was .87 (P<.0002); for the number of comments received .86 (p<.0003); and for total comments (initiated plus received) .90 (p<.0000).

Because ranked data would be used in the data analysis, the number of comments should also be rank ordered within each group and compared using the ranked data. In this case, Spearman rank-order correlations could be used to compare the rankings of data for each coder. The correlations of the ranking of the initiated comments score were .98 (p<.0000), and for the received comments .98 (p<.0000), and for the ranking of the total comments score (initiated plus received comments) 1.00 (p<.0000).

Convergent Validity

Construct validity of the process measure of opinion leadership can be determined by the convergence of the process approach with other measures of opinion leadership. As specified by Campbell & Fiske (1959), different measures of the same concept must demonstrate a relationship.

	Childers OL Scale	# Total Comments	# Comments Initiated	# Comments Received
Childers Scale	x			
# Total Comments	.11 (243) .0800	x		
# Comments Intiated	.14 (243) .0239	.88 (243) .0001	x	
# Comments received	.13 (243) .0506	.86 (243) .0001	.70 (243) .0001	x
Dogmatism	.07 (243) n.s.	-.08 (243) n.s.	-.05 (243) n.s.	-.07 (243) n.s.

Table 8: Self-Report Scale vs Process Measure

The strength of the validation depends on using methodologically dissimilar measures. In the example, we show a comparison of data from three different measures of opinion leadership: a frequently used self-report opinion leadership scale (Childers, 1986) by which each subject assesses his/her own level of opinion leadership; the process measure of opinion leadership, e.g., total comments (initiated and received comments), determined by a content analysis of group discussions; and a sociometric measure of subjects' ratings of other group members (as to group leader, most influential group member, and least influential group member).

The groups were operationalized as follows: the predicted opinion leaders (individuals highest in cognitive complexity) were assigned to groups discussing product purchases and use. After the discussions, the groups rated each member in terms of group leadership and influence.

The Spearman correlations above present a comparison of the rankings of the self-report scores and the process scores for 243 subjects.

	Process Measure:		Self-Designating Scale:	
	Highest # Comments	Lowest # Comments	Highest Score	Lowest score
Sociometric Measure:				
Subject who acted as group leader	119	14	67	57
Subject who influenced me the most	91	10	48	50
Subject who influenced me the least	11	81	25	63

Table 9: Comparing 3 Opinion Leadership Measures

The correlations of the self-designating scale and the process measure of opinion leadership (# total comments) provide only slight evidence of convergent validity. The self-designating scale appears significantly correlated with one process component (# comments initiated) within the .05 level of significance. The correlations of the opinion leadership scale with process elements (total comments and # comments received) are significant and below a .10 level.

When we compare results of the process measure of opinion leadership with the sociometric opinion leadership ratings (e.g., each group member rating the other members within their discussion group), things begin to look much clearer.

In Table 9 you see the power of the observational or process measure to identify opinion leaders while the standard and much used Childers (1986) self-report scale appears unable to distinguish between opinion leaders and non-leaders.

The sociometric ratings of group members were elicited at the end of each group discussion. The group members rated each other as to "the subject who acted as the group leader," and "subject who influenced me most," and "the subject who influenced me least." The comparison of these ratings and the process measure is shown in table 9 above.

Table 9 shows amazing results. When we compare the subject ratings of other group members' influence, a total of 91 individuals who were named as most influential also reflected the highest ranked total comments score. The same is true for the 119 subjects who were named as group leader; they also were ranked highest in total number of comments.

Only 10 individuals identified as most influential reflected the lowest ranked total scores. Similarly, only 14 individuals who were named as group leader ranked lowest in number of comments.

In contrast, about an equal number of individuals with the highest and lowest ranked self-designating opinion leadership scale scores were identified as most influential by group members. Again, about an equal number of subjects with the highest and lowest *self-designating scores* were ranked as group leader. The frequently used Childers (1986) self-designating instrument failed to differentiate between opinion leaders and non-leaders, when compared to the sociometric group ratings and the observational or process measure results.

In psychometric terms, it appears that convergent validity is evident for the process measure of opinion leadership. The self-designating scale, on the other hand, appears to lack convergent validity. In effect, a coin toss would result in about the same results generated by the Childers (1986) opinion leadership self-designating scale.

In virtually all cases, the predicted opinion leaders, the individuals with the highest cognitive complexity scores, were the same individuals identified as the group opinion leader by their group members.

Nomological Validity

Nomological validity demonstrates that there is a relationship among related concepts. We can show nomological validity when our theoretical set of constructs correctly predicts other relationships. In this case, the set of personality variables associated with cognitive complexity provides the theoretical basis for predicting the identity of opinion leaders within the small group setting.

	Self-Designating Scale	Total # Comments	# Comments Initiated	# Comments Received
Cognitive Complexity	.14 .0357	.18 .0042	.17 .0086	.21 .0010
Abstract Thinking	.11 .0785	.17 .0092	.18 .0053	.23 .0002
Ambiguity Tolerance	.18 .0052	.06 n.s.	.007 n.s.	.18 .0058
Empathy	.02 n.s.	.03 n.s.	.03 n.s.	-.001 n.s.
Affective Communication	.16 .0120	.29 .0001	.31 .0001	.18 .0054
Product Interest	-.05 n.s.	-.03 n.s.	-.03 n.s.	-.03 n.s.
Product Knowledge	.04 n.s.	.03 n.s.	.09 n.s.	-.01 n.s.

Table 10: Correlations of Opinion Leadership Measures & Traits

With reference to Table 10 appearing above, the nomological validity (e.g., the predicted relationship) of the opinion leadership measures appears evident for three of the variables: cognitive complexity, abstract thinking, and affective communication– for which the correlations are all positive and significant.

In general, the nomological validity of the process measure appears greater, in both magnitude and significance, than the self-designating opinion leadership scale.

Discriminant Validity

For a new measure, it should demonstrate that it is also unrelated to scales measuring dissimilar constructs. For example, we looked to see if there was any correlation between opinion leadership and dogmatism, a concept associated with a tendency to be authoritative and dictatorial, and therefore uncaring about people and their reactions.

Dogmatism should be unrelated to measures of opinion leadership which are based on an affinity for people and a desire to assist others with recommendations and information. As expected, the components of the process measure show a greater correspondence with each other than with the results of a scale measuring dogmatism.

Summary

We started this chapter with several short biographical sketches of opinion leaders whom we admire, followed by some brief comments and conclusions about who they and what they do and have accomplished.

We describe a new process measure of opinion leadership that was calculated by observing and recording group discussions and then using the Bales et al (1951) Interaction Matrix technique to rank order group members according to the total comments they initiated and received during the product-related discussions.

To assess the quality of this procedure, we looked at the interrelater reliability, convergent validity, nomological validity, and discriminant validity tests that were performed.

The results of the observational or process measure (total ranked comments) which predicted the identities of the opinion leader in each group, closely agreed with the sociometric ratings (by which each group member indicated the group members they thought acted as group leader, and the group members who influenced them the most and the least). The results confirmed that the observational method of identifying opinion leaders was extremely accurate. Equally important, cognitive complexity, abstract thinking, and expressiveness also identified opinion leaders extremely well.

The Childers (1986) self-designating opinion leadership scale performed poorly. It was correct in identifying opinion leaders only about 50% of the time, about the same probability as tossing a coin.

Thus, we judged the self-designating method of identifying opinion leaders to be less reliable than the observational method, e.g., process measure, or by the prediction of opinion leadership by related cognitive personality traits.

Action Steps

In your opinion, why does the observational measure of opinion leadership perform so well, while the self-report measure identifies opinion leaders accurately only 50% of the time?

CHAPTER

WHO ARE THE INFLUENCERS?

Elizabeth Gurdian-Gonzalez

Figure 28: Before/After Photos

Losing 138 pounds on the Keto diet is quite an accomplishment all by itself. But what is so remarkable about Elizabeth Gurdian-Gonzalez is that she became the founder of an online Facebook community dedicated to the Keto diet lifestyle. The group has now grown to over 540 members!

Elizabeth is an inspiration to hundreds of people who subscribe to her Facebook page where they can chat directly with Liz and ask her advice about everything from recipes and menus to grocery store shopping and even vacation preferences. Liz also conducts free online sessions about various topics of interest.

Elizabeth is a veritable cornucopia of information about healthy living. Her suggestions help people achieve lasting weight loss, and how to succeed and embrace a thin and healthy lifestyle.

Former Vice President Al Gore

Figure 29: A Campaign Using Opinion Leaders

It was reported that former Vice President, Al Gore, made use of the multi-step opinion leadership model for his Climate Project, hiring environmentally savvy individuals to espouse his concerns about climate change. He started a viral word-of-mouth campaign by using opinion leaders to spread the word.

Before Gore's efforts, the public was indifferent to climate issues. What Gore did was to figure a way to bring his message directly to people in all walks of life who would "buy in" to climate problems. Those opinion leaders, in turn, would use word-of-mouth channels to influence family members, friends, and colleagues. This was a strategy that had a cascading influential effect (History.com, 2019; Wikipedia).

In a recent article about climate change and opinion leadership, Nisbet & Kotcher (2009) noted that opinion leaders could popularize the need for country-wide policy changes and to change consumer consumption to reduce carbon emissions.

The strategy of using opinion leaders to disseminate climate issues was clearly successful and certainly helped Gore's selection as a recipient of both the Academy Award and 2007 Nobel Peace Prize for the documentary, *An Inconvenient Truth* (History.com, 2019; Wikipedia).

Margaret Bradford

Figure 30: A Champion for Newborns

Before Margaret Bradford's second son, Gavin was born, the hospital staff had spotted several problems during the ultrasound exam, including a serious congenital heart defect. This ultimately led to open heart surgery at Akron General Hospital to rebuild one wall separating two chambers within Gavin's heart.

Margaret discovered that congenital heart disease (CHD) is the most common type of birth defect and that it affects one out of every 100 babies born in the United States.

Although a simple, non-evasive procedure exists to diagnose CHD, many states did not require such testing for newborns and many of these newborns were sent home where they died. Margaret immediately started a Facebook page and became an outspoken advocate for newborn testing, resulting in interviews by Fox news and in giving testimony before state legislatures.

All states now require mandatory CHD testing of newborns. Besides educating hundreds of families directly, Margaret has undoubtedly played a role in helping to save thousands of newborns' lives.

Amber Faust

Figure 31: A Family-Oriented Influencer

Amber Faust is a professional photographer who loves taking – and posting - photos of her adorable kids. Who would have guessed that her skill + interest would have turned into a successful and growing influencer business? With the added benefit of living on Hilton Head Island, with its beautiful beaches, scenery, and seascapes, Amber discovered the perfect combination of elements that contribute to her being a sought-after online influencer.

Amber hadn't planned to become an influencer representing various products and services that are (photographed with) and used by her children. She had some 50,000 followers before she realized that her online activities were no longer just a hobby! Already a talented, professional photographer, she has had to learn all about Instagram and blogging, and how to depend on her own unique talents and skills, to set her apart from other social media influencers.

Being an influencer has turned out to be a wonderful life, giving her an abundant amount of time to enjoy being with her kids.

Because of her efforts, she and her children have been sent to Paris and to Disney World for photo shoots. Besides all of this, Amber manages both her online business demands, and being an active mom and wife to her busy firefighter husband.

These "Ordinary" Influencers

We can make some observations about the people we have identified above as influencers:

1) In each case, their promotional activities draw people to them.
2) They are generally followed by large numbers of people who value what they say or do. Often, their comments are "retweeted" by their followers.
3) They are fully engaged with people on a regular basis. If they slack off for any reason (vacation, illness, etc.), the group activity immediately diminishes.
4) They are public figures and often occupy a central position within the community. Their influence affects people far and wide within their own network.
5) In addition to engaging in product-related communications with others, influencers provide non-verbal cues through personal "branding" that enhances the images of the products they represent.
6) The major activity of influencers occurs on social media sites via comments, blogs, podcasts, tweets, and advertisements, where they can influence many people simultaneously.
7) Gore's own role, as a former VP and public figure, means he is a celebrity influencer.

By using the Personal Construct Theory of Opinion Leadership for guidance, we can also predict online influencers' characteristics, and choose methods for determining their identities. While opinion leaders communicate via in-person, face-to-face interactions, Influencers are primarily active in social media networks such as Facebook, Instagram, YouTube, or Twitter, where they disseminate information by communicating through internet technology, rather than in-person.

›

Since social media sites do not require face-to-face contact, influencers need not possess either the cognitive nor verbal communication characteristics that opinion leaders must have to influence others in the offline world.

In the online world, "everyone's an Influencer" (Bakshy, 2011). Given that anyone can tweet or comment online, the Individuals who dispense information and opinions online may not be opinion leaders, however, they can easily act as influencers.

For Influencers, an abundance of product knowledge is easily accessed online, and an interest for a topic of interest can arise quickly when needed. In the online social media world, *offline opinion followers* have become, in fact, *online influencers.* Like offline opinion followers, influencers can be cognitively simple and concrete, prefer certainty, act self-interestedly, and be less effective in face-to-face encounters.

Let's look at one social media influencer. His name is Ralphie Waplington, and he represents several companies and their products in the UK. He was recently described in the New Yorker magazine as Britain's youngest social media influencer (Scott, 2019). He is 2 years old.

We can be quite confident that Ralphie has not yet fine-tuned his cognitive personality traits, nor communication skills, which would allow him to be verbally persuasive and convincing. Clearly, Ralphie is an Influencer, not an opinion leader.

There are significant differences between opinion leaders and online influencers. The following table summarizes the major ones that you should remember:

	Opinion Leaders	Online Influencers
Personal Construct Opinion Leadership Theory traits (Cognitive Complexity, Abstract Thinking, Ambiguity Tolerance, Empathy, Expressiveness, etc.)	Yes, these traits determine opinion leader personality, as well as the ability to act as opinion leaders during face-to-face interactions	No, influencers do not require these traits since they operate online rather than face-to-face; influencers may be opinion followers offline
Influence Over Multiple Product Categories	Yes, opinion leadership traits empower opinion leaders to act across diverse product categories	No, influencers tend to specialize in specific product areas according to their sponsor companies, e.g., baby/toddler products & toys, electronics, fashion & jewelry, etc.
High Level of Product Knowledge & Interest	No, knowledge and interest are not prerequisites for opinion leadership behavior; opinion leaders can self-generate information; they can also discern topical information during word-of-mouth interactions	Yes, influencers often become experts in the categories in which they operate, reflecting high levels of knowledge and interest. They can access information quickly, and filter that data before online use is necessary

Table 11: Opinion Leaders V›s. Online Influencers

Identifying Influencers

The existence of online influencers is a potent reminder that a huge number of product-related discussions, comments, and endorsements now occur on the internet. For millennials, and Gen Z and other demographic groups, social media has emerged as the preferred source of news and information, rather than face-to-face sources or traditional broadcast media.

The amount of interpersonal activity among social media members can be tracked with existing analytics and software packages

(Winter & Neubaum, 2016). This tracking ability has produced several metrics that identify influencer nodes, either as senders or recipients of interpersonal influence, within specific networks, including Facebook pages, tweets, videos, blogs, podcasts, etc.

Other statistical approaches, such as measures of centrality, and Leader and Page ranking algorithms, are being used to identify those individuals involved in the greatest amount of interpersonal activity. Although sometimes supplemented by an analysis of the most thought-provoking tweets or messages (Spranger, et al, 2018), the major determinant of influencer importance is simply the number of their followers.

The number of individuals on social media who can act as either influencers or followers is rather staggering. Facebook alone has almost 2 billion users. Instagram has 1 billion monthly users. Twitter is also one of the world's largest social networks with some 330 million users each month. On YouTube, almost 5 billion videos are watched each day. It is the 2nd most visited site in the world. "On an average day, eight out of ten 18-49-year-olds watch YouTube" (Smith & Anderson, 2019).

According to a recent study by InfluenceDB (2019), there are over 500,000 active influencers on Instagram alone. That totals about 39% of all Instagram accounts having over 15,000 followers. About 81% of this active influencer group have followers numbering between 15,000 to 100,000 users (Droesch, 2019).

InfluencerMarketingHub indicates that Influencer marketing has grown from $1.7B in 2017, to a projected $6.5B in 2019. The top 50 Instagram influencers have 3.1 billion followers. Instagram influencers receive payments from corporate sponsors ranging from free products to over $1 million annually.

INFLUENCER TIERS	# FOLLOWERS
Celebrity Influencers	5 Million +
Mega Influencers	1 Million – 5 Million
Macro Influencers	500K - 1 Million
Mid-Tier Influencers	50K – 500K
Micro Influencers	10K – 50K
Nano Influencers	1K – 10K

Table 12: Influencer Tiers

A breakdown of six different influencer tiers, defined by numbers of followers, according to MediaKix, appear in Table 12.

Selena Gomez	$550,000 per post
Kim Kardashian	$500,000 per post
Cristiano Ronaldo	$400,000 per post
Kyle Jenner	$400,000 per post
Kendell Jenner	$370,000 per post

Table 13: Celebrity Influencers

The highest earning celebrity influencers are shown in Table 13 (Cagnoni,2018).

According to the InfluencerMarketingHub, ordinary individuals who are macro-influencers, e.g., who become tastemakers and trendsetters, command high, but not astronomical, fees. Influencer compensation can be a flat rate fee for each published item of content, or a combination based on sales and click-throughs (Wikipedia).

Influencer Marketing

Most large companies today include some of their marketing budgets for influencer marketing. Surveys at InfluencerMarketingHub have seen an increase in influencer marketing from 37% of companies surveyed in 2017 to 86% by 2019.

IZEA Discovery (2019) suggests that it may be advantageous for companies to manage their influencer marketing campaigns with an in-house team. The benefits include control over strategy, determination of the best methods for identifying and contacting potential influencers, building state-of-the-art key performance indicator (KPI) data analytics, and compliance with legal requirements, an area of growing concern.

The main objective is to find the right influencers for one's brand. These are influencers whose followers are similar to the individuals within the brand's target market (InfluencerMarketingHub).

Finding the right influencers can be a time-consuming and difficult process. Even with centrality software, this is a function that can no longer be done manually or unsystematically. A basic approach for identifying influencers can be described as follows:

1. Choose a community that focuses on a given topic
2. Determine the interpersonal relationships (information flows and exchanges) among members
3. Produce a sociogram or visual representation of the information flows
4. Identify the central players in the community by using social network analysis methods (e.g., centrality software)

Figure 32: Identifying Online Influencers
(Adapted from Plotkowiak, 2012)

Most companies either use agencies specializing in identifying online influencers, or software platforms, that will match the company's brands with the appropriate influencers in order to gain online exposure and sales.

There are a multitude of companies that offer methods and services geared to locating the influencers that meet a company's brand and corporate needs. The next section will discuss several of the major commercial approaches – selected on the basis of market presence - that are currently available.

Influencer Marketing Platforms

AspireIQ is generally acknowledged as being one of the leading platforms for identifying online influencers (Skinner, 2018; InfluencerMarketingHub, 2019). It provides access to 2 million plus influencers using its search engine dashboard, and direct access to influencers, and real-time analytics. The company provides a website that offers an abundance of information, including free downloadable eBooks (*The Ultimate Guide to Influencers, How Much to Pay Instagram Influencers,* and *Influence Generated Content is Key to Facebook Ads Success*). There are also numerous case studies, Infogram best practices, and succinct one-page guides to help jump start the process.

AspireIQ services include the ability to create custom content for each marketing channel, use of their self-service platform, as well as fully managed campaigns.

Upfluence is another influencer platform that includes a focus on bloggers. Their clients include Swiss Army products, PayPal, Nestle, Citroen, and Air France.

Their platforms include Reachr which finds influencers among the thousands of bloggers in over 200 industries listed in Upfluence's database. The platform provides over 50 filters to adjust one's search, and the ability to contact influencers directly and negotiate contracts via the platform. The company indicates that it takes about 16 minutes to identify influencers with the Upfluence platform. Clients can also contact designers for new creatives via Upfluence's Publishr platform (InfluencerMarketingHub.com).

IZEA, which began in 2006, was among the early platforms that targeted bloggers to obtain sponsored content for its clientele. According to InfluencerMarketingHub.com, *IZEA*'s platform uses a host of filters to identify influencers according to market demographics, subject matter, keywords, social channels, etc.

Figure 33: IZEAx 3.0 Enterprise Influencer Platform

The company also compiles listings of content creators, writers, photographers, graphic designers and videographers (InfluencerMarketingHub.com).

IZEA searchers can find influencers on various channels, including Facebook, Instagram, Twitter, Tumblr, YouTube, WordPress, and other blogs. *IZEA's* clients include Whole Foods, eBay, Google, and Walmart.

Collective Bias has been named one of Forbes' Most Promising Companies for three years in a row. It boasts a hand-selected community of 10,000+ shopping-focused influencers with an aggregate multichannel reach of over 80 Million online consumers. Much of the company's strength is presumably derived from being a wholly owned subsidiary of Inmar, Inc., a consumer-oriented technology company with well-known coupon, prescription, and product return software applications.

The company uses proprietary data technologies to enable influencer selection and management. In 2018, *Collective Bias* became the first company to offer pricing based on verified exposures to Instagram content, so clients only pay for the exposures they actually receive on Instagram. This innovation falls in line with the company's pledge of complete transparency in its performance. Even if influencers try to inflate their value, the company is guaranteeing that all impressions are 100 percent viewed and verified, thus reducing influencer marketing risks substantially for its clientele.

Linqia Marketing, another company marketing to influencers, uses a platform driven by artificial intelligence. It predicts and guarantees the results for each of its influencer marketing programs. According to *Linqia's* website, its influencer "discovery engine continually crawls the internet, analyzing hundreds of data points across millions of potential influencers to identify the best performers." *Linqia's* database contains 100,000 influencers who currently meet its performance criteria. The company also indicates that its Performance Platform utilizes machine learning that identifies influencer and brand affinities, thus assuring patterns that predict greater campaign success.

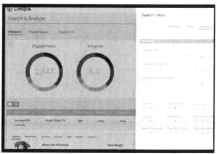

Figure 34: Linqia Influencer Marketing Platform

As indicated earlier, influencer marketing has now grown into a $6.5B industry. We can conclude from above that internet companies have wisely chosen to pursue online influencers rather than online opinion leaders.

Using the Personal Construct Theory of Opinion Leadership for guidance, we address the subject of identifying online opinion leaders in the next section.

131

"Wherefore Art Thou, Online Opinion Leaders?"

No doubt, there are opinion leaders who are active online and who do their share of influencing other people. But trying to find them is like trying to find a needle in a haystack.

Plotkowiak (2012) suggests that hashtags could be assessed by content to identify opinion leaders or influentials according to their specific markets and segments. Several online services, such as "wefollow.com" and "twellow.com," categorize Twitter tags which facilitate this approach. He also notes that such hashtag topic lists can be overwhelming, requiring additional effort to extract and sort tags into larger and more useful categories.

Most efforts to identify social media opinion leaders use a variety of software algorithms that compute "centrality" (zeroing in on the key sources of network influence (such as information flows and activity) and "rankings" (calculating the positions of social network participants). Spanger et al (2018), for example, have employed centrality measures which assess the number of outgoing messages or activity that network members generate.

Similarly, Lee et al (2010) conducted two online opinion leadership studies which reported correlations for two measures of centrality and two measures of opinion leadership (the latter from a self-report instrument as well as from member ratings of friendship or closeness). The results appear mixed, with some correlations appearing significant, while others were insignificant.

Lee et al (2010) suggest that opinion leadership appears to be affected by whether individuals perceive and can judge themselves and others as "popular." This is an interesting comment given that online popularity is a determinant of influencers, and not necessarily of opinion leadership.

Trying to identify online opinion leaders is fraught with other problems. For example, while investigating the micro-blogging activity on Twitter, in an attempt to identify opinion leader influence, Weng et al (2010) observed that almost 75% of the active individuals on Twitter reciprocally follow about 80% of their own followers.

Under these circumstances, opinion leaders cannot be distinguished from opinion followers (or non-leaders). The interaction reciprocity that Weng et al (2009) observed means that everyone on Twitter has the potential to be an influencer!

The same observation is emphasized by Bakshy et al (2011) in a research article entitled, *Everyone's an influencer: Quantifying Influence on Twitter.* The researchers investigated the relative influence of 1.6 million Twitter users, observing that "the largest [information] cascades tended to be generated by users who have been influential in the past and who have a large number of followers." They conclude that

> "The Twitter ecosystem is also well suited to studying the role of influencers ...Twitter is expressly devoted to disseminating information, in that *users subscribe to broadcasts of other users*" [emphasis added].

Walter & Bruggem (2018) similarly realized that "opportunity makes opinion leaders," by allowing opinion leaders to obtain first-hand information via social media networks. Their research acknowledges the fact that individuals no longer need to rely on information provided by mass media sources, since all social media users have access to first-hand online information."

In other words, information is available to everyone, and everyone can act as an online influencer! The ability to distinguish online opinion leaders from online followers has become inextricably blurred. No doubt research that tries to identify online opinion leaders will continue, but in a somewhat otiose fashion.

Summary

The Personal Construct Theory of Opinion Leadership explains the fact that:

- in the offline environment, the individuals who disseminate information and influence are opinion leaders;
- in an online, or social media environment, the individuals providing information and advice are influencers.

The Influencers' technological position, which includes access to online information, obviates the importance of the personality and communication traits normally associated with opinion leadership in the offline world. Many offline opinion followers have migrated to the online sphere, where they can become successful online influencers.

Identifying and reaching online influencers is relatively straight-forward and uncomplicated. Numerous online platforms now provide companies with access to influencers, who exert a great deal of influence within desired markets and segments.

Action Steps

Go back to the beginning of Chapters 7 and 8 and review the biographies of the individuals identified as opinion leaders and influencers. What determines if an individual is an opinion leader or an influencer? Can someone act as both an influencer and an opinion leader? Under what circumstances would companies choose to market to opinion leaders? And to influencers?

CHAPTER 9

PRODUCT KNOWLEDGE AND INTEREST

Most studies of influentials assume that opinion leaders and influencers influence others by virtue of their greater knowledge and interest in some specific product category or topic.

For determining the product knowledge and interest levels of opinion leaders, scores for product interest and knowledge were derived from two questions asked in discussion groups for each of several products (answering service, yogurt, microwave oven, soup, cameras, banking, pain relievers, music, and TV):

Concerning this product grouping,
I would describe myself as:

Interested   6...5...4...3...2...1   Uninterested

Knowledgeable 6...5...4...3...2...1 Unknowledgeable

Figure 35: Product Knowledge & Interest Scales

In looking back at Table 10 in chapter 7 (on page 113), we note that the correlations of product knowledge and interest scores were non-significant with respect to measures of opinion leadership.

Therefore, we saw no relationship between opinion leadership and product interest and knowledge. How can that be?

Having found opinion leaders to be cognitively complex, we can turn to the existing cognitive complexity literature to get a preliminary idea about the lack of association of product interest or knowledge and opinion leadership. We find that cognitively complex individuals have been shown to self-generate information often independent of external stimuli (Scott, 1962; Bieri et al, 1975).

Cognitively complex individuals appear to understand phenomena, even if they lack specific information or details. Consequently, their opinion leadership behavior is not limited to situations of product familiarity or salience (Bieri & Blacker, 1956; Zajonc, 1968). Such individuals, therefore, still exhibit a propensity to engage in product related conversations regardless of the product knowledge or interest they might have about a particular product category. In other words, opinion leadership can easily extend across multiple product categories.

To explore the relationship of opinion leadership, cognitive complexity, and product interest and knowledge more fully, we used loglinear models to detect any significant associations among the variables in question. This was appropriate given the group design that gave us the product-oriented discussions and the rank order data derived from those recorded interactions.

In this section of the book we will look at the relationship of the individuals' group ranked scores for the four major variables: the Bieri measure of cognitive complexity (RBieri); the individuals' ranked opinion leadership observational, process measure, e.g., the total interpersonal comments generated and received during group discussions (Rtotal); the amount of the participants' ranked product interest scores (RInterest); and the amount of the participants' ranked product knowledge scores (RKnow).

Cognitive Complexity & Product Knowledge/Interest

Log Linear Models	DF	Chi-Square	Prob.
Rtotal*Rbieri	8	23.48	.0028
Rtotal*Rbieri*Rknow	26	44.97	.0119
Rtotal*Rbieri*Rinterest	26	45.93	.0093
Rtotal*Rbieri*Rknow*Rinterest	63	83.97	.0399

Table 14: Cognitive Complexity Loglinear Models

The first table above summarizes four models created and analyzed using the loglinear procedures in SAS (Statistical Analysis System) for 243 participants in 52 discussion groups. The statistical results are from an unpublished study conducted by the author some years ago. As real-life examples, they are included here to illustrate how the model explains opinion leadership behavior.

The initial statistics indicate the chi-square significance for each of the log-linear models. Although the models of cognitive complexity and opinion leadership appear significant, knowledge or interest moderate the relationship between opinion leadership and cognitive complexity to a limited degree.

Rtotal*Rbieri

Obs	Rtotal	Rbieri	Rknow	Rinterest	Chi Square	Prob.
43	1	1			12.05	.0005
37	2	1			5.41	.0200
16	2	3			4.09	.0432

Table 15: Opinion Leadership & Cognitive Complexity

The pattern of frequencies for the first model (Rtotal*Rbieri) indicates that participants high in cognitive complexity also reflect either high or moderate levels of opinion leadership. Note that the scores are ranked as follows: 1=high, 2=moderate, and 3=low for all variables.

The cell reflecting cognitively simple (score=3)/ moderately high opinion leaders (score=2) is significantly lower than was expected by chance, and thus agrees with the predicted relationship (e.g., individuals low in cognitive complexity would not act, in general, as opinion leaders).

Rtotal*Rbieri*Rknow

Obs	Rtotal	Rbieri	Rknow	Rinterest	Chi Square	Prob.
19	1	1	2		13.58	.0002
15	1	2	1		5.72	.0167
14	2	1	1		4.24	.0395
17	2	1	2		9.29	0023

Table 16: Opinion Leadership, Cognitive Complexity & Knowledge

When product knowledge is added to the model, the association of cognitive complexity and opinion leadership is significant but reflects fewer observations. Thus, the association of cognitive complexity and opinion leadership is not strengthened by product knowledge.

Rtotal*Rbieri*Rinterest

Obs	Rtotal	Rbieri	Rknow	Rinterest	Chi Square	Prob.
16	1	1		1	7.87	.0050
17	1	1		2	9.81	.0017
15	1	2		2	6,13	.0133
16	2	1		1	7.87	.0050
14	2	2		1	4.58	.0324
2	2	3		1	4.03	.0448

Table 17: Opinion Leadership, Cognitive Complexity & Interest

The pattern observed in the second model is also reflected in the third model where the effects of product interest are included. In this case, the cell of cognitively simple/moderately high opinion leaders also reflects fewer individuals than would be expected by chance. When the rbieri score = 3 (low), a frequency of only 2 participants reflected moderate (rtotal=2) opinion leadership scores. As expected, we would not expect cognitively simple individuals to act as opinion leaders.

Rtotal*Rbieri*Rknow*Rinterest

Obs.	Rtotal	Rbieri	Rknow	Rinterest	Chi Square	Prob.
8	1	1	1	1	7.63	.0058
7	1	1	2	3	5.02	.0250
8	1	1	3	3	7,63	.0058
7	1	2	1	1	5.02	.0250
7	1	2	1	2	5.02	.0250
7	1	3	1	1	5.02	.0250
12	2	1	1	1	22.17	.0001
7	2	1	2	2	5.02	.0250
9	2	2	1	1	10.68	.0011
8	3	1	1	1	7.63	.0058

Table 18: Opinion Leadership, Complexity, Knowledge/Interest

In the complete or fully saturated model (including the effects of both product knowledge and product interest), the pattern of predicted findings is largely reiterated (for 8 of 10 significant cells). In two cells, subjects appear high in cognitive complexity and opinion leadership, despite low levels of product knowledge and product interest. These cells follow other studies that have found that individuals display behaviors associated with cognitive complexity even when the amount of external information is limited (Bieri & Blacker, 1956; Richmond 1977).

In two cells, the results are contrary to predictions. In one cell, for example, cognitively simple individuals appear high in opinion leadership, product knowledge, and product interest. A likely interpretation of this finding is that product interest and product knowledge may allow the cognitively simple or concrete individual to overcome interpersonal limitations and thus assume the opinion leadership role. Thus. product interest and product knowledge may be more important to non-leaders than for opinion leaders.

Abstract Thinking & Product Knowledge/Interest
(n=243)

Log Linear Models	DF	Chi-Square	Prob.
Rtotal*Rabstract	8	25.55	.0013
Rtotal*Rabstract*Rknow	26	48.20	.0050
Rtotal*Rabstract*Rinterest	26	38.41	.0554
Rtotal*Rabstract*Rknow*Rinterest	66	90.76	.0234

Table 19: Abstract Thinking Loglinear Models

The Personal Construct Model of Opinion Leadership also posits that abstract thinking (a variable closely related to cognitive complexity) is also predictive of opinion leadership. In this section, we will review the Loglinear models depicting the relationship of abstract thinking and opinion leadership, and product knowledge and product interest.

The initial statistics indicate the chi-square significance for each of the log-linear models. As indicated in the above table, the individual model testing the effects of product interest is not significant at the .05 level. Once again, knowledge or interest moderate the relationship between opinion leadership and abstract thinking to a limited degree.

In Table 20, the significant participant frequencies for the first model depict the relationship between opinion leadership and abstract thinking. Once again, the scores are ranked as follows: 1=high, 2=moderate, and 3=low for all variables.

In the first model, the number of opinion leaders who exhibit either high or moderately high levels of abstract thinking is significantly greater than those expected by chance. In addition, opinion leaders who reflect concrete thinking are also fewer in number than would be expected as a random occurrence.

Rtotal*Rabstract

Obs	Rtotal	Rabstract	Rknow	Rinterest	Chi Square	Prob
41	1	1			9.44	.0021
42	1	2			10.03	.0011
16	1	3			4.15	.0417

Table 20: Opinion Leadership & Abstract Thinking

Similar findings are also evident in the 2nd model which includes the subjects' self-ratings of product knowledge. In Table 21, the association of opinion leadership with either high or moderate levels of abstract thinking is evident. The number of opinion leaders who appear to be concrete thinkers is significantly lower in number than would be expected by chance. The last significant cell of this model depicts the individuals who appear moderate in opinion leadership, low in abstract thinking, and high in product knowledge. Thus, it would appear that product knowledge may act as a compensatory factor, empowering concrete thinkers who ordinarily lack the personality dimensions required to act as an opinion leader.

Rtotal*Rabstract*Rknow

Obs	Rtotal	Rabstract	Rknow	Rinterest	Chi Square	Prob
15	1	1	2		6.02	.0141
19	1	2	1		14.05	.0002
14	1	2	2		4.49	.0341
2	1	3	3		4.06	.0439
15	2	3	1		6.02	.0141

Table 21: Opinion Leadership, Abstract Thinking & Knowledge

In the full model, shown in Table 21, individuals who are either high or moderately high in opinion leadership are also characterized by abstract thinking, and by high or moderate levels of product interest and product knowledge. In one cell, however, individuals who appear high in both opinion leadership and abstract thinking evidence low levels of product knowledge and interest.

Based on these indications, product knowledge and interest may have a limited or negligible influence on the behavior of the cognitively abstract opinion leaders within our sample of group participants.

An additional cell reflects an incidence of subjects characterized as cognitively concrete, moderately high opinion leaders. Notably, these individuals have high self-rated levels of product interest and knowledge. Possibly, product interest and knowledge equip cognitively concrete individuals with the motivation or ability to serve as opinion leaders. This explanation suggests that the moderating effects of product knowledge and interest have a greater effect on the potential opinion leadership activities of concrete individuals than on abstract ones.

Rtotal*Rabstract*Rknow*Rinterest

Obs	Rtotal	Rabstract	Rknow	Rinterest	Chi Square	Prob
8	1	1	1	1	8.14	.0043
7	1	1	3	3	5.41	.0200
10	1	2	1	1	14.92	.0001
9	2	1	1	1	11.32	.0003
7	2	1	2	2	5.41	.0200
8	2	2	2	2	6.14	.0043
10	2	3	1	1	14.92	.0001
9	3	1	1	1	11.32	.0008

Table 22: Opinion Leadership, Abstract Thinking, Knowledge & Interest

In Table 22, the final significant cell in the total model depicts individuals who did not act as opinion leaders, despite having high levels of abstract thinking, product knowledge, and product interest. Similar to the results obtained for cognitive complexity, this finding suggests that other factors may affect the propensity to act as opinion leaders in certain situations. Evidently, cognitively abstract individuals may be dissuaded from acting as opinion leaders when confronted by group situations or dynamics that appear risky, unclear and/or inauspicious.

Ambiguity Tolerance & Product Knowledge & Interest

Loglinear Models	Df	Chi Square	Prob
Rtotal*Rambig	8	17.01	.0300
Rtotal*Rambig*Rknow	26	41.07	.0306
Rtotal*Rambig*Rinterest	26	28.09	.0620
Rtotal*Rambig*Rknow*Rinterest	63	77.77	.0977

Table 23: Ambiguity Tolerance Loglinear Models

In Table 23, a significant relationship is indicated between opinion leadership and ambiguity tolerance, as shown in the first (main effects) model in the table. Adding product knowledge as a moderating variable does not appear to influence the main relationship to any extent. In addition, the models that include product interest appear to be insignificant at the .05 level.

Rtotal*Rambig					
Obs	Rtotal	Rambig	Rknow	Chi Sq.	Prob.
43	1	1		11.10	.0009
17	3	2		4.66	.0558

Table 24: Opinion Leadership & Ambiguity Tolerance

In the first model in Table 24, Rtotal *Rambig, the average expected cell size is 27. Thus, the first significant cell in the table reflects a greater number of high ambiguity tolerant, opinion leaders than would be expected by chance. At the same time, non-leaders who display moderate levels of ambiguity tolerance also appear to be fewer in number than by chance expectation.

Rtotal*Rambig*Rknow

Obs	Rtotal	Rambig	Rknow	Chi Sq.	Prob.
20	1	1	2	16.89	.0001
15	1	3	1	6.30	.0121
14	2	2	2	4.73	.0296
1	2	3	3	4.53	.0334
2	3	2	2	3.95	.0470

Table 25: Opinion Leadership, Ambiguity Tolerance & Knowledge

In Table 25, a significantly high number of ambiguity tolerant opinion leaders again appears evident in the second loglinear model. In addition, there are significantly fewer opinion leaders reflecting low levels of ambiguity tolerance and product knowledge than would be expected by chance. Similarly, the number of non-leaders exhibiting moderate ambiguity tolerance levels is also significantly fewer than would be expected by chance.

Notably, one cell consists of opinion leaders whose low levels of ambiguity tolerance appears to be offset by high product knowledge. These subjects suggest that product knowledge may moderate the behavior of individuals low in ambiguity tolerance rather than those who are ranked high on this characteristic.

Empathy & Product Knowledge/Interest

Loglinear Models	Df	Chi Square	Prob
Rtotal*Remp	8	19.46	.0166
Rtotal*Remp*Rknow	26	43.43	.0174
Rtotal*Remp*Rinterest	26	56.30	.0005
Rtotal*Remp*Rknow*Rinterest	63	96.47	.0043

Table 26: Empathy Loglinear Models

We turn next to the results for empathy and its association with opinion leadership. The loglinear models specifying a relationship between empathy and opinion leadership appear significant. Since the models appear meaningful, the significant response frequencies of each model have been summarized in the tables that follow.

Cell #1 of the first model, in Table 27, shows a concentration of individuals who appear high both in opinion leadership and in empathy. No other cells appear significant in the first model.

Rtotal*Remp

Obs	Rtotal	Remp	Rknow	Rinterest	Chi Sq.	Prob.
42	1	1			19.46	.0126

Table 27: Opinion Leadership & Empathy

In Table 28, three of the four cells in the second model reflect patterns which are in accord with predictions: a group of subjects with high levels of opinion leadership, empathy, and product knowledge; another group, ranked mid-range in opinion leadership, and high in both empathy and product knowledge; and a third

Rtotal*Remp*Rknow

Obs	Rtotal	Remp	Rknow	Rinterest	Chi Sq.	Prob.
21	1	1	1		18.57	.0001
10	1	3	2		4.27	.0388
14	2	1	1		4.27	.0388
2	2	3	3		4.15	.0417

Table 28: Opinion Leadership, Empathy & Product Knowledge

group, a cell of predictably fewer individuals, exhibiting low levels of empathy and product knowledge, and moderate levels of opinion leadership. Contrary to expectations, one cell in the model appears to comprise opinion leaders (high rtotal) who reflected low empathy and moderate knowledge rankings.

In most cells in the third model (Table 28), opinion leadership reflects high or moderate rankings of empathy and interest. Results in two cells are contrary to expectations, with opinion leaders reflecting low levels of empathy and interest, and non-leaders reflecting high levels of empathy and interest. In addition to some empathy scale issues, empathy may not perform as reliably as cognitive complexity and abstract thinking in discerning opinion leadership.

Rtotal*Remp*Rinterest

Obs	Rtotal	Remp	Rknow	Rinterest	Chi Sq.	Prob.
19	1	1		1	26.24	.0001
15	1	1		2	6.82	.0090
15	2	2		2	6.82	.0090
15	1	3		3	6.82	.0090
16	2	1		2	8.66	.0033
16	3	1		1	8.66	.0033
1	3	3		2	4.41	.0358

Table 29: Opinion Leadership, Empathy & Interest

In the fourth model (Table 29), which includes the effects of both product knowledge and product interest, the predicted pattern of relationships between opinion leadership and empathy occurs in 5 of the 7 significant cells. Only one cell performed contrary to expectations.

Rtotal*Remp*Rknow*Rinterest

Obs	Rtotal	Remp	Rknow	Rinterest	Chi Sq.	Prob.
13	1	1	1	1	26.24	.0001
7	1	1	1	2	4.86	.0275
7	1	3	2	3	4.86	.0275
10	2	1	1	1	13.83	.0002
9	2	1	1	2	10.42	.0012
7	2	2	1	1	4.86	.0275
12	3	1	1	1	21.77	.0001

Table 30: Opinion Leadership, Empathy, Knowledge & Interest

In Table 30, the last group, which reflects high empathy – high knowledge, and high-interest non-leaders, reflects the earlier observation that non-leaders can act as opinion leaders, inasmuch as knowledge and interest appear to compensate for the low levels of traits that opinion leaders usually have.

However, empathy by itself may not perform as strongly as other variables in the model. Possibly this variable may be affected by other influences, including scale construction, group composition, etc.

Expressiveness & Product Knowledge/Interest

Loglinear Models	Df	Chi Square	Prob
Rtotal*Rexp	8	29.84	.0002
Rtotal*Rexp*Rknow	26	53.07	.0013
Rtotal*Rexp*Rinterest	26	47.72	.0058
Rtotal*Rexp*Rknow*Rinterest	67	104.97	.0021

Table 31: Expressiveness Loglinear Models
(n=243)

The loglinear models specifying a relationship between expressiveness and opinion leadership appear significant. Accordingly, the significant response frequencies are summarized below.

Rtotal*Rexp

Obs	Rtotal	Rexp	Rknow	Rinterest	Chi Sq.	Prob.
49	1	1			19.46	.0126
16	1	3			4.40	.0446
16	3	1			4.40	.0446

Table 32: Opinion Leadership & Expressiveness

In the first model in Table 32, the cell of expressive opinion leaders is significantly higher than that expected by chance, while the cells of expressive non-leaders, and non-expressive leaders, are significantly lower than chance expectancies. These cells support the theory's predicted associations.

Rtotal*Rexp*Rknow

Obs	Rtotal	Rexp	Rknow	Rinterest	Chi Sq.	Prob.
21	1	1	1		19.38	.0001
14	1	1	2		4.61	.0318
14	1	1	3		4.61	.0318
15	1	2	2		6.16	.0141
15	2	1	1		6.16	.0131
15	2	2	2		6.16	.0131

Table 33: Opinion Leadership, Expressiveness & Knowledge

In Table 33, all cells in the 2nd model are significantly higher than expected for random events. All three levels of product knowledge occur with expressive opinion leaders. In one cell, a low level of product knowledge appears with a high level of opinion leadership (Rtotal), and high expressiveness (Rexp). Overall, product knowledge does not appear to be a significant factor in the occurrence of opinion leadership.

In the third model, shown in Table 34, the opinion leadership, expressiveness relationship is reiterated. In line with the theory's predictions, one cell of expressive non-leaders is significantly smaller than expected by chance. In addition, there does not appear to be any consistent association between expressiveness and product interest.

Rtotal*Rexp*Rinterest						
Obs	Rtotal	Rexp	Rknow	Rinterest	Chi Sq	Prob.
22	1	1		1	21,62	.0001
14	1	1		2	4,40	.0359
14	2	1		1	4.40	.0359
14	2	2		2	4.40	.0359
2	3	1		2	4.10	.0430

Table 34: Opinion Leadership, Expressiveness & Interest

In the fourth fully saturated model, summarized in Table 35, expressiveness appears associated with opinion leadership. In one cell of moderate opinion leadership, a low degree of expressiveness appears counteracted by high levels of product knowledge and product interest. The cells of expressive opinion leaders with low levels of product knowledge and product interest suggest a lack of need for these variables by highly expressive individuals. Thus, the need for product knowledge and product interest may be greater situationally by enabling non-expressive individuals who act as opinion leaders.

Rtotal*Rexp*Rknow*Rinterest

Obs	Rtotal	Rexp	Rknow	Rinterest	Chi Sq.	Prob.
15	1	1	1	1	19.54	.0001
8	1	1	3	3	8.64	.0034
7	1	2	2	2	5.80	.0160
10	2	1	1	1	15.67	.0001
7	2	3	2	2	11.94	.0005
7	3	1	1	1	5.80	.0160
7	3	3	1	1	5,80	.0160

Table 35: Opinion Leadership, Expressiveness, Know. & Interest

"Hit Rates"

Based on the Personal Construct Model of Opinion Leadership introduced in Chapter Two, we would predict that group participants with the highest level of cognitive complexity and highest total comments scores would be identified as the individuals who acted as opinion leaders during the group discussion of products and services. According to the process measure of opinion leadership, it was predicted that these individuals would have initiated and received the greatest number of comments during group discussions.

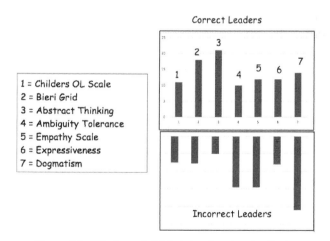

1 = Childers OL Scale
2 = Bieri Grid
3 = Abstract Thinking
4 = Ambiguity Tolerance
5 = Empathy Scale
6 = Expressiveness
7 = Dogmatism

Figure 36: "Hit Rates" Of Opinion Leaders by Traits

It should be noted that individuals correctly classified as opinion leaders would include only those individuals with the highest scores on the variables shown from the model. In addition to cognitive complexity, for example, only individuals who reflected the highest abstract scores and highest total comments would be correctly classified as opinion leaders. The same approach was used to compute "hit rates" or correctly chosen opinion leaders for each of the remaining model variables.

A visual inspection of Figure 38 shows that two variables (cognitive complexity and abstract thinking) performed well in predicting the identity of opinion leaders. That is, they identified the greatest number of opinion leaders correctly (as measured by the process measure of opinion leadership) and they identified fewer individuals incorrectly.

In addition, the two variables correctly identified approx. 60% to 90% more opinion leaders, respectively, than did the self-designating opinion leadership scale. The following discussion will focus exclusively on cognitive complexity and abstract thinking.

Specifically, eighteen individuals were correctly identified as opinion leaders based on having been ranked highest within their groups on the Bieri measure of cognitive complexity. The probability that the 18 correct classifications could have occurred by chance is negligible (p<.0000).

Only 7 opinion leaders appeared to be cognitively simple (lowest Rbieri). An examination to their Bieri scores, however, revealed that 4 of the 7 actually had mid-range scores and that only 3 opinion leaders were actually cognitively simple. Thus, in only 3 out of 52 groups did cognitively simple individuals act as opinion leaders.

From the earlier Loglinear analyses, it appeared that cognitively simple individuals who assumed the role of opinion leader also exhibited high levels of product knowledge and interest, indicating that these factors may have strengthened their ability to serve as an opinion leader, thus, overcoming personality deficiencies that otherwise prevented them from acting in that capacity previously.

The number of correct non-leaders (those ranked lowest on the Bieri measure) totaled 21. Thus, in 21 of the 52 groups, the individual ranked lowest in cognitive complexity also was ranked lowest in opinion leadership. Of the non-leaders (lowest Rtotal scores), only 6 represent misclassifications reflecting high levels of cognitive complexity (high Rbieri score). These individuals may not have acted as opinion leaders due to situational considerations, such as lack of group cohesion and cooperation, interpersonal antipathy, or other factors.

Summary

This chapter examined the relationship between opinion leadership, product knowledge, product interest, and other model variables, e.g., cognitive complexity, abstract thinking, ambiguity tolerance, empathy, and expressiveness.

As suggested by the Personal Construct Theory of Opinion Leadership, there appears to be little correlation between opinion leadership and product knowledge and interest. Thus, this chapter corrects the generally accepted assumption that opinion leaders reflect high product knowledge and product interest. There is also very little association between the other model variables and product knowledge and interest.

In a similar fashion, online influencers do not appear to require product knowledge or interest when disseminating information, since this occurs electronically rather than face-to-face. The information is readily available to influencers when needed. They need not exhibit the personality dimensions which opinion leadership requires in direct, person-to-person exchanges.

This chapter demonstrates that some individuals can act as opinion leaders, even though they exhibit low levels of cognitive complexity, abstract thinking ability, and other traits. As predicted by the Personal Construct Theory of Opinion Leadership, such individuals have high levels of product knowledge and product interest that, essentially, compensate them for the absence of the personality dimensions that opinion leaders ordinarily need.

Notably, the "hit rates," or classifications of group members as opinion leaders by group participants found that only 3 out of 52 groups (6 %) had individuals acting as opinion leaders who were cognitively simple or concrete. Usually these individuals reflected moderate or high levels of product knowledge and interest. Cognitive complexity and abstract thinking were evident in 94% of the groups' opinion leaders.

Some of the conceptual variables, such as leadership orientation and charisma, were added to complete the model's theoretical framework. Future analyses can confirm the compensatory role of product knowledge and product interest regarding non-opinion leaders who act in an opinion leadership position.

Action Steps

Let's assume that you are a financial consultant who is hired by a large jewelry retail company to advise employees about their 401K retirement plans. The jewelry company is hopeful that you will be able to convince employees to increase participation in the plan About 40% of the employees (particularly the new and younger workers) do not participate in the plan, and the company is hoping to get total participation closer to 100%.

You immediately notice that you appear to have a considerable amount of competition when it comes to giving employees sound financial advice.

A good number of employees apparently seek out financial guidance from several individuals who work as diamond cutters in the diamond room.

These diamond cutters are extremely well trained, and they tend to be somewhat older than other workers. Cutting diamonds means that the individual possesses a considerable amount of knowledge, and skill, and that he/she is responsible for handling inventories that can range into the millions of dollars.

You came prepared to present several seminars to all of the employees, urging them to increase their rate of participation. However, you are now uncertain if that is the best strategy to follow.

Based on your knowledge of opinion leadership, what changes in consulting strategy must you make in order to be successful?

What did you learn from this exercise?

REFERENCES

8 Influencer Marketing Platforms to Amplify your Campaigns. (2019, May 15). Retrieved June 11, 2019, from https:// influencer marketinghub.com

Allport, G. W. (1937) Personality, New York: Holt, Rinehart & Winston, 286-342.

Allport, G. W. (1960). *Personality and social encounter*. Boston: Beacon.

Allport, G. W. (1961). *Pattern and growth in personality*. New York: Holt, Rinehart and Winston.

Alvy, K.T. (1973). The Development of Listener-Adapted Communications in Grade School Children From Different Social Class Backgrounds, Genetic Psychology Monographs February 87 (1), 33-104.

Anderson, C., Keltner, D., & John, O. P. (2003). Emotional convergence between people over time. *Journal of Personality and Social Psychology, 84*(5), 1054-1068. doi:10.1037/0022-3514.84.5.1054

Antonakis, J. (2014). Predictors of Leadership: The Usual Suspects and the Suspect Traits. In A. Bryman (Author), *The SAGE handbook of leadership*. Los Angeles: SAGE.

AspireIQ. (2019). The Leading Influencer Marketing Platform. http://aspireiq.com/

Bakshy, E., Hofman, J. M., Mason, W. A., & Watts, D. J. (2011). Everyone's an influencer. *Proceedings of the Fourth ACM International Conference on Web Search and Data Mining - WSDM '11*.

Baldwin, D. A., Greene, J. N., Plank, R. E., & Branch, G. E. (1996). Compu-Grid: A Windows-Based Software Program for Repertory Grid Analysis. *Educational and Psychological Measurement, 56*(5), 828-832.

Bales, R. F. (1970). *Personality and interpersonal behavior*. New York: Holt, Rinehart and Winston.

Bales, R. F., Strodtbeck, F. L., Mills, T. M., & Rosenborough, M. E. (1951). Channels of Communication in Small Groups. *American Sociological Review, 16*(4), 461.

Bannister, R. (1957). *The four minute mile; illustrated with photos*. New York: Dodd, Mead.

Bartels, B. L., & Mutz, D. C. (2009). Explaining Processes of Institutional Opinion Leadership. *The Journal of Politics, 71*(1), 249-261

Bartunek, J. M., Gordon, J. R., & Weathersby, R. P. (1983). Developing "Complicated" Understanding in Administrators. *The Academy of Management Review, 8*(2), 273.

Bass, B. M. (1990). From transactional to transformational leadership: Learning to share the vision. *Organizational Dynamics, 18*(3), 19-31.

Bauer, R. (1981). Consumer Behavior as Rick Taking. In *Dynamic marketing for a changing world; proceedings of the 43rd National Conference of the American Marketing Association, June 15, 16, 17, 1960* (pp. 389-398).

Baumgartner, H. (2002). Toward a Personology of the Consumer. *Journal of Consumer Research, 29*(2), 286-292.

Bean-Mellinger, B. (2019). Differences Between Task-Oriented Leaders & Relational Oriented Leaders, 2019. www. smallbusiness.chron.com

Bearden, W. O., Netemeyer, R. G., & Teel, J. E. (1989). Measurement of Consumer Susceptibility to Interpersonal Influence. *Journal of Consumer Research, 15*(4), 473.

Beatty, M. J. (1998). Trait Research. In J. C. McCroskey (Author), *Communication and personality: Trait perspectives*. Cresskill, NJ: Hampton Press.

Beatty, M. J., & Pascual-Ferra, P. (2016). Trait Theories. In K. B. Jensen, R. T. Craig, J. Pooley, & E. W. Rothenbuhler (Authors), *The international encyclopedia of communication theory and philosophy*. John Wiley & Sons.

Belk, R.W. (1971). Occurrence of Word-of-Mouth Buyer Behavior as a Function of Situation and Advertising Stimuli. In F.C. Allvine (Ed.), Proceedings (419-422). Chicago: American Marketing Association

Bertrandias, L., & Goldsmith, R. E. (2006). Some psychological motivations for fashion opinion leadership and fashion opinion seeking. *Journal of Fashion Marketing and Management: An International Journal, 10*(1), 25-40.

Bieri, J. (1955). Cognitive complexity-simplicity and predictive behavior. *The Journal of Abnormal and Social Psychology, 51*(2), 263-268.

Bieri, J., & Blacker, E. (1956). The generality of cognitive complexity in the perception of people and inkblots. *The Journal of Abnormal and Social Psychology, 53*(1), 112-117.

Bieri, J., Atkins, A. L., Briar, S., Leaman, R. L., Miller, H., & Tripodi, T. (1975). *Clinical and social judgment: The discrimination of behavioral information*. Huntington, NY: R.E. Krieger Pub.

Blair, R. (2005). Responding to the emotions of others: Dissociating forms of empathy through the study of typical and psychiatric populations. *Consciousness and Cognition, 14*(4), 698-718.

Bono, J. E., & Ilies, R. (2006). Charisma, positive emotions and mood contagion. *The Leadership Quarterly, 17*(4), 317-334.

Borba, M. (2017). *Unselfie: Why empathetic kids succeed in our all-about-me world*. New York: Touchstone.

Brendel, W., & Bennett, C. (2016). Learning to Embody Leadership Through Mindfulness and Somatics Practice. *Advances in Developing Human Resources, 18*(3), 409-425.

Brett, J. E., & Kernaleguen, A. (1975). Perceptual and Personality Variables Related to Opinion Leadership in Fashion. *Perceptual and Motor Skills, 40*(3), 775-779.

Brilhart, J. K. (1988). Observing and Evaluating Discussions. In R. S. Cathcart, L. A. Samovar, & L. D. Henman (Eds.), *Small group communication: Theory & practice*. Madison: Brown & Benchmark.

Brooker, G., & Houston, M. J. (1976). An Evaluation of Measures of Opinion Leadership. Proceedings of the American Marketing Association, Chicago.

Build Closer Relationships With the Right Opinion Leaders. (n.d.). https://www.monone 11, 2019, cl.com/solutions/medical-affairs/

Burleson, R. R., & Caplan, S. E. (1998). Cognitive Complexity. In J. C. MacCroskey (Author), *Communication and personality: Trait perspectives*. Hampton Press.

Burson-Marsteller EMEA, B. (n.d.). E-Fluentials: The Power of Online Influencers. https://issuu.com/burson-marsteller-emea/docs/e-fluentials_brochure

Cagnoni, G. (2018, May 03). Top 10: The highest-paid influencers on Instagram in 2017. https://www.blogmeter.eu/blog-en/20a., 18/05/02/

Cai, L.A., Feng, R. & Breiter, D. (2004). Tourist purchase decision involvement and information preferences. Journal of Vacation Marketing.

Campbell, D. T., & Fiske, D. W. (1959). Convergent and discriminant validation by the multitrait-multimethod matrix. *Psychological Bulletin, 56*(2), 81-105.

Chan, K. K., & Misra, S. (1990). Characteristics of the Opinion Leader: A New Dimension. *Journal of Advertising, 19*(3), 53-60.

Chaney, I. M. (2001). Opinion leaders as a segment for marketing communications. *Marketing Intelligence & Planning, 19*(5), 302-308.

Chaudhry, S. A. (2013). Opinion Leadership and its Role in Buyer Decision Making, Academy of Contemporary Research Journal 7(1) 7-14.

Childers, T. L. (1986). Assessment of the Psychometric Properties of an Opinion Leadership Scale. *Journal of Marketing Research, 23*(2), 184.

Chlopan, B. E., McCain, M. L., Carbonell, J. L., & Hagen, R. L. (1985). Empathy: Review of available measures. *Journal of Personality and Social Psychology, 48*(3), 635-653.

Choi, S. (2014). The Two-Step Flow of Communication in Twitter-Based Public Forums. *Social Science Computer Review, 33*(6), 696-711.

Collective Bias. (2019). Collective Bias | An Inmar Influencer Marketing Agency. https://www.collectivebias.com/

Conger, J. A., Kanungo, R. N., & Menon, S. T. (2000). Charismatic Leadership And Follower Effects. *Journal of Organizational Behavior, 21*(7), 747-765.

Covey, S.R. & Gulledge, K. A. (1992), Principle-Centered Leadership. Journal for Quality and Participation, (July/August).

Crant, J. M., & Bateman, T. S. (2000). Charismatic leadership viewed from above: The impact of proactive personality. *Journal of Organizational Behavior, 21*(1), 63-75.

Crockett, W. H. (1965). Cognitive Complexity and Impression Formation. In B. A. Maher & C. W. Backman (Eds.), *Progress in experimental personality research* (pp. 47-90). New York: Academic Press.

Darr, C., Barko, J., & Robinson, B. (2004). *Putting online Influentials to work for your campaign*. Washington, D.C.: Institute for Politics, Democracy & the Internet.

Davis, M. H. (1983). Measuring individual differences in empathy: Evidence for a multidimensional approach. *Journal of Personality and Social Psychology, 44*(1), 113-126.

Dawar, N., Parker, P. M., & Price, L. J. (1996). A Cross-Cultural Study of Interpersonal Information Exchange. *Journal of International Business Studies, 27*(3), 497-516.

DeGaulle, C. (1960). *The edge of the sword*. New York: Criterion Books.

Delia, J. G., & Clark, R. A. (1977). Cognitive complexity, social perception, and the development of listener-adapted communication in six-, eight-, ten-, and twelve-year-old boys. *Communication Monographs, 44*(4), 326-345.

Delia, J. G., Clark, R. A., & Switzer, D. E. (1974). Cognitive complexity and impression formation in informal social interaction. *Speech Monographs, 41*(4), 299-308.

Delwiche, A. (n.d.). Agenda–setting, opinion leadership, and the world of Web logs. Retrieved June 13, 2019, from https://journals.uic.edug.php/fm/article/view/1300

Dillon, W. R., Madden, T. J., & Firtile, N. H. (2004). *Marketing research in a marketing environment*. Illinois: Irwin.

Droesch, B. (2019, March 05). Is Everyone on Instagram an Influencer? https://www.emarketer.com

Duan, C., & Hill, C. E. (1996). The current state of empathy research. *Journal of Counseling Psychology, 43*(3), 261-274.

Duhachek, A., & Iacobucci, D. (2005). Consumer Personality and Coping: Testing Rival Theories of Process. *Journal of Consumer Psychology, 15*(1), 52-63.

Durand, R. M. (1978). Cognitive Complexity and the Perception of Attitude Objects: An Examination of Halo Error. *Perceptual and Motor Skills, 46*(3_suppl), 1235-1239.

Durand, R.M. & Arie, O.G. (1980). Cognitive Differentiation: A Moderator of Behavioral Intentions in Proceedings of the 1980 American Marketing Association Educators' Conference, Series No. 46, 305-308.

Dweck, C. S., & Leggett, E. L. (1988). A social-cognitive approach to motivation and personality. *Psychological Review, 95*(2), 256-273.

Eisenberg, N., & Miller, P. A. (1987). The relation of empathy to prosocial and related behaviors. *Psychological Bulletin, 101*(1), 91-119

Ferdinand Tonnies: Public opinion. (1991).
www.DigitalResearch@Fordham.

Fransella, F., & Bannister, D. (1977). *BA Manual for Repertory Grid Techniques By Fay Fransella and Don Bannister*. London.: Academic Press.

Frenkel-Brunswik, E. (1949). Intolerance Of Ambiguity As An Emotional And Perceptual Personality Variable. *Journal of Personality, 18*(1), 108-143.

Friedman, H. S., Prince, L. M., Riggio, R. E., & Dimatteo, M. R. (1980). Understanding and assessing nonverbal expressiveness: The Affective Communication Test. *Journal of Personality and Social Psychology, 39*(2), 333-351.

Friedman, M. S. (2012). *Martin Buber: The Life of Dialogue*. London: Routledge.

Furnham, A., & Marks, J. (2013). Tolerance of Ambiguity: A Review of the Recent Literature. *Psychology, 04*(09), 717-728.

Förster, J., Friedman, R. S., & Liberman, N. (2004). Temporal Construal Effects on Abstract and Concrete Thinking: Consequences for Insight and Creative Cognition. *Journal of Personality and Social Psychology, 87*(2), 177-189.

Gallese, V. (2003). The Roots of Empathy: The Shared Manifold Hypothesis and the Neural Basis of Intersubjectivity. *Psychopathology, 36*(4), 171-180.

Gardner, R. W., & Schoen, R. A. (1962). Differentiation and abstraction in concept formation. *Psychological Monographs: General and Applied, 76*(41), 1-21.

Garrod, S., & Pickering, M. J. (2004). Why is conversation so easy? *Trends in Cognitive Sciences, 8*(1), 8-11.

Gaw, B. A. (1976). The Johari window and a partnership: An approach to teaching interpersonal communication skills.

Gnambs, T., & Batinic, B. (2012). The Roots of Interpersonal Influence: A Mediated Moderation Model for Knowledge and Traits as Predictors of Opinion Leadership. *Applied Psychology, 62*(4), 597-618.

Goldenberg, J., Han, S., Lehmann, D. R., & Hong, J. W. (2009). The Role of Hubs in the Adoption Process. *Journal of Marketing, 73*(2), 1-13.

Goldsmith, R. E., & Witt, T. S. (2003). The Predictive Validity of an Opinion Leadership Scale. *Journal of Marketing Theory and Practice, 11*(1), 28-35.

Goldsmith, R. E., Flynn, L. R., & Goldsmith, E. B. (2003). Innovative Consumers and Market Mavens. *Journal of Marketing Theory and Practice, 11*(4), 54-65.

Goleman, D. (1986, December 2). Major Personality Study Finds That Traits are mostly Inherited. *The New York Times*.

Gottman, J. M., & Silver, N. (2018). *The seven principles for making marriage work*. London: Cassell Illustrated.

Graff, J., & Darr, C. (2004). Political Influentials Online in the 2004 Presidential Campaign, Institute for Politics & The Internet, George Washington University

Greene, J. N. (1990). *Cognitive complexity and the prediction of opinion leadership communication behavior* (Unpublished doctoral dissertation). City University of New York Graduate Center.

Grewal, R., Mehta, R., & Kardes, F. R. (2000). The role of the social-identity function of attitudes in consumer innovativeness and opinion leadership. *Journal of Economic Psychology, 21*(3), 233-252.

Gross, E. J. (1971). Katz and Lazarsfeld Revisited: And Possibly Upended. *Journal of Marketing Research, 8*(1), 131.

Hale, C. L. (1980). Cognitive complexity-simplicity as a determinant of communication effectiveness. *Communication Monographs, 47*(4), 304-311.

Hale, C. L., & Delia, J. G. (1976). Cognitive complexity and social perspective-taking. *Communication Monographs, 43*(3), 195-203.

Hill, J. (2017). Abstract Vs. Concrete Language. Motlow Community College, Smyrna, TN. www.mscc.edu

History, channel. "Al Gore Wins Nobel Prize in the Wake of An Inconvenient Truth – 2007." *The Burning Platform*, 12 Oct. 2017, www.theburningplatform.com

Hogan, R. (1969) Development of an Empathy Scale. Journal of Consulting and Clinical Psychology 33(3) 307-316.

Holmes, D. D., & Edmondson, A. (2000). *The Johari Window*. Cincinnati, OH: Diana Duncan Holmes.

Horvath, C. W. (1998). Biological origins of Communicator Style. In J. C. McCroskey (Author), *Communication and personality: Trait perspectives*. Cresskill, N.J: Hampton Press.

House, R. J., & Aditya, R. N. (1997). The Social Scientific Study of Leadership: Quo Vadis? *Journal of Management, 23*(3), 409-473.

How is Social Media Playing the Role of an Opinion Leader Today (March 6, 2011). www.mccollins-media.com.

Huang, C., Lien, L., Chen, P., Tseng, T., & Lin, S. (2017). Identification of Opinion Leaders and Followers in Social Media. *Proceedings of the 6th International Conference on Data Science, Technology and Applications*.

Huckfeldt, R. (2001). The Social Communication of Political Expertise. *American Journal of Political Science, 45*(2), 425.

Hudson, R. (1974). Images of the Retailing Environment: An Example of the Repertory Grid Methodology. *Environment and Behavior, 6*(4), 470-494.

Huhn, R., Ferreira, J. B., Freitas, A. S., & Leão, F. (2018). The effects of social media opinion leaders' recommendations on followers' intention to buy. *Review of Business Management, 20*(1), 57-73.

In Communication Models, G. (2014, July 10). The Johari Window Model. Retrieved June, 2019, from https://www.communicationtheory.org

Influencer Marketing Hub | How-To Guides, Influencer Platform Reviews & Agency Case Studies. (n.d.). https://influencermarketinghub.com/

Influencer marketing. (2019, June 04). Retrieved June 11, 2019, from https://en.m.wikipedia.org

InfluencerDB. (2019, May 13). State of the Industry – Influencer Marketing in 2019. https://blog.influencerdb.com

Influencing the Influencers: How Online Advertising and Media Impact Word of Mouth (2006). www.doubleClick.com

Iyengar, R., Bulte, C. V., & Valente, T. W. (2011). Opinion Leadership and Social Contagion in New Product Diffusion. *Marketing Science, 30*(2), 195-212.

Iyengar, R., Han, S., & Gupta, S. (2009). Do Friends Influence Purchases in a Social Network? *SSRN Electronic Journal*.

IZEA. (2019, May 02). Building an In-House Influencer Team: What You Need to Know. https://qa.izea.com

Jensen, K. B., Craig, R. T., Pooley, J., & Rothenbuhler, E. W. (2016). Trait Theories. In *The international encyclopedia of communication theory and philosophy*. John Wiley & Sons.

Jin, Y., Bloch, P., & Cameron, G.T. (2002). A Comparative Study: Does the Word-of-Mouth and Opinion Leadership Model Fit Epinions on the Internet? https://www.researchgate.net

Judge, T. A., Colbert, A. E., & Ilies, R. (2004). Intelligence and Leadership: A Quantitative Review and Test of Theoretical Propositions. *Journal of Applied Psychology, 89*(3), 542-552.

Kallet, M. (2014). Headscratchers and Critical Thinking. Retrieved June, 2019, from http://www.headscratchers.com/

Kallet, M. (2014). *Think smarter: Critical thinking to improve problem-solving and decision-making skills*. Hoboken, NJ: Wiley.

Kaplan, A. M., & Haenlein, M. (2011). Two hearts in three-quarter time: How to waltz the social media/viral marketing dance. *Business Horizons, 54*(3), 253-263.

Kassarjian, H. H. (1971). Personality and Consumer Behavior: A Review. *Journal of Marketing Research, 8*(4), 409. doi:10.2307/3150229

Katz, E., & Lazarsfeld, P. F. (1955). *Personal influence: The part played by people in the flow of mass communications*. Glencoe: Free Press.

Keller, E. B., & Berry, J. L. (2003). *The influentials*. New York: Free Press.

Kelly, G. (1955). *The psychology of personal constructs*. New York: W. W. Norton.

Kim, H., & Hong, H. (2011). Fashion Leadership and Hedonic Shopping Motivations of Female Consumers. *Clothing and Textiles Research Journal, 29*(4), 314-330.

King, C. W., & Summers, J. O. (1970). Overlap of Opinion Leadership across Consumer Product Categories. *Journal of Marketing Research, 7*(1), 43-50.

Kramer, K., & Gawlick, M. (2003). *Martin Buber's I and thou: Practicing living dialogue*. New York: Paulist Press.

Kramer, P. K. (2012). Martin Buber's Spirituality: Hassidic Wisdom for Everyday Life. Rowman & Littlefield

Kuhn, T. S. (2015). *The structure of scientific revolutions*. Chicago, IL: The University of Chicago Press.

Lam, S. S., & Schaubroeck, J. (2000). A field experiment testing frontline opinion leaders as change agents. *Journal of Applied Psychology, 85*(6), 987-995.

Lawrence, E. J., Shaw, P., Baker, D., Baron-Cohen, S., & David, A. S. (2004). Measuring empathy: Reliability and validity of the Empathy Quotient. *Psychological Medicine, 34*(5), 911-920.

Lazarsfeld, P. F., Berelson, B., & Gaudet, H. (1948). *The People's Choice*. Columbia University Press.

Lee, S. H., Cotte, J., & Noseworthy, T. J. (2010). The role of network centrality in the flow of consumer influence. *Journal of Consumer Psychology, 20*(1), 66-77.

Lennon, S. J., & Davis, L. L. (1987). Individual Differences in Fashion Orientation and Cognitive Complexity. *Perceptual and Motor Skills, 64*(1), 327-330.

Levenson, R. W., & Ruef, A. M. (1992). Empathy: A physiological substrate. *Journal of Personality and Social Psychology, 63*(2), 234-246.

Lewin, K. (n.d.). Psychology and the process of group living. *The Complete Social Scientist: A Kurt Lewin Reader.,* 333-345.

Linqia. (2019). Performance-based Influencer Marketing. https://linqia.com/

Livingstone, S. (2006). The Influence of Personal Influence on the Study of Audiences. *The ANNALS of the American Academy of Political and Social Science, 608*(1), 233-250.

Lopes, P. et al, (2004). Emotional Intelligence and Social Interaction, Personality and Social Psychology Bulletin, 1018-1034

Lyons, B., & Henderson, K. (2005). Opinion leadership in a computer-mediated environment. *Journal of Consumer Behavior, 4*(5), 319-329.

Madupu, V. & O'Cooley, D. (2007). Comprehension of Metaphors in Advertisements: Opinion Leaders versus Non-Opinion Leaders. *Society For Marketing Advances*, Proceedings, 24-27.

Marcus, A. S., & Bauer, R. A. (1964). Yes: There Are Generalized Opinion Leaders. *Public Opinion Quarterly, 28*(4), 628. doi:10.1086/267286

Maven Seven Network Research Inc. (2013, January 03). Social Media and the Power of Networks- Key Opinion Leaders on Twitter. Retrieved June 11, 2019, from https://www.socialmediatoday.com/content

McCroskey, J. C., & Daly, J. A. (1986). *Personality and interpersonal communication*. Beverly Hills, CA: Sage Publications.

Mill, J. S. (2002). *On Liberty*. Dover Publications.

Montgomery, D. B., & Silk, A. J. (1970). *Clusters of consumer interests and spheres of influence of opinion leaders*. Cambridge: M.I.T.

Morita, M., Kondō, A., & LeVine, P. (1998). *Morita therapy and the true nature of anxiety based disorders (Shinkeishitsu)*. Albany, NY: State University of New York Press.

Muneno, R., & Dembo, M. H. (1982). Causal Attributions for Student Performance. *Personality and Social Psychology Bulletin, 8*(2), 201-207.

Myers, J. H., & Robertson, T. S. (1972). Dimensions of Opinion Leadership. *Journal of Marketing Research, 9*(1), 41.

Nicosia, F. M. (1964). Opinion Leadership and the Flow of Communication: Some Problems and Prospects. In *Proceedings of the Fall Conference: Reflections on Progress in Marketing, Ed. L. G. Smith* (pp. 340-358). Chicago: American Marketing Association.

Nieuwenhuis, R., Groten, M. T., & Pelzer, B. (2016). Influence.ME: Tools for Detecting Influential Data in Mixed Effects Models.

Nisbet, E. C. (2006). The Engagement Model of Opinion Leadership: Testing Validity Within a European Context. *International Journal of Public Opinion Research, 18*(1), 3-30.

Nisbet, M. C., & Kotcher, J. E. (2009). A Two-Step Flow of Influence? *Science Communication, 30*(3), 328-354.

Norton, R. W. (1975). Measurement of Ambiguity Tolerance. *Journal of Personality Assessment, 39*(6), 607-619.

O'keefe, B. J., & Delia, J. G. (1978). Construct Comprehensiveness and Cognitive Complexity. *Perceptual and Motor Skills, 46*(2), 548-550.

O'keefe, B. J., & Delia, J. G. (1979). Construct comprehensiveness and cognitive complexity as predictors of the number and strategic adaptation of arguments and appeals in a persuasive message. *Communication Monographs, 46*(4), 231-240.

O'keefe, D. J., Shepherd, G. J., & Streeter, T. (1982). Role category questionnaire measures of cognitive complexity: Reliability and comparability of alternative forms. *Central States Speech Journal, 33*(1), 333-338.

Parker, R. L. (1972). A Comparison of Two Approaches To The Measurement of Cognitive Complexity in an Impression Formation Task with Congruent and Incongruent Stimuli. Unpublished doctoral dissertation. Temple University.

Pescosolido, A. T. (2002). Emergent leaders as managers of group emotion. *The Leadership Quarterly, 13*(5), 583-599.

Phillips, D. (1993, February 01). Lincoln on Leadership: Executive Strategies for Tough Times. https://www.amazon.com/Lincoln-Leadership-Executive-Strategies-Tough/dp/0446394599

Plotkowiak, T. (2012, April 17). How to make sense out of Twitter tags. https://twitterresearcher.wordpress.com/

Pooley, J. (2006). Fifteen Pages that Shook the Field: Personal Influence, Edward Shils, and the Remembered History of Mass Communication Research. *The ANNALS of the American Academy of Political and Social Science, 608*(1), 130-156.

Popova, M. (2018, April 07). I and Thou: Philosopher Martin Buber on the Art of Relationship and What Makes Us Real to One Another. https://www.brainpickings.org

Reingen, P. H., & Kernan, J. B. (1986). Analysis of Referral Networks in Marketing: Methods and Illustration. *Journal of Marketing Research, 23*(4), 370-378.

Reynolds, D. K. (1976). *Morita psychotherapy*. Berkeley: University of California Press.

Reynolds, F. D., & Darden, W. R. (1971). Mutually Adaptive Effects of Interpersonal Communication. *Journal of Marketing Research, 8*(4), 449.

Richins, L., M., & Root-Shaffer,T. (1988, January 01). The Role of Evolvement and Opinion Leadership in Consumer Word-Of-Mouth: An Implicit Model Made Explicit. http://www.acrwebsite.org/search/view-conference-proceedings.aspx?Id=6790

Richmond, V. P. (1977). The Relationship Between Opinion Leadership And Information Acquisition. *Human Communication Research, 4*(1), 38-43.

Robertson, T. S., & Myers, J. H. (1969). Personality Correlates of Opinion Leadership and Innovative Buying Behavior. *Journal of Marketing Research, 6*(2), 164-168.

Roch, C. H. (2005). The Dual Roots of Opinion Leadership. *The Journal of Politics, 67*(1), 110-131.

Rogers, E. M. (1976). New Product Adoption and Diffusion. *Journal of Consumer Research, 2*(4), 290.

Rogers, E. M., & Cartano, D. G. (1962). Methods of Measuring Opinion Leadership. *Public Opinion Quarterly, 26*(3), 435.

Ross, I. (1975, January 01). Perceived Risk and Consumer Behavior: A Critical Review. http://www.acrwebsite.org/volumes/5741/volumes/v02/NA-02

Row, H. (2006, December). - Influencing the Influencers: How Online Advertising and Media Influence Word of Mouth. https://www.artsmanagement.net/articles

S. (2015, December). Opinion-Leader in Marketing: Definition & Explanation.

Sager, N. (n.d.). Tolerance For Ambiguity as a Gateway to Leadership Opportunity. https://mathias-sager.com/

Saito, K., Teramoto T., and Inoue, A.(2015). How opinion leaders are made by the social media. Ad Studies, Vol 52

Sajuria, J., Vanheerde-Hudson, J., Hudson, D., Dasandi, N., & Theocharis, Y. (2014). Tweeting Alone? An Analysis of Bridging and Bonding Social Capital in Online Networks. *American Politics Research, 43*(4), 708-738.

Schachinger, M. (1991). *Ferdinand Tönnies: Public opinion*.

Schiffman, L. G., & Wisenblit, J. (2019). *Consumer behavior*. Harlow, England: Pearson.

Schroder, H. M., & Suedfeld, H. P. (1971). Cognitive complexity and personality organization. In *Personality theory and information processing*. New York: Ronald Press.

Schroder, H. M., Streufert, S., & Driver, M. J. (1967). *Human information processing: Individuals and groups functioning in complex social situations*. New York: Holt, Rinehart and Winston.

Scott, L. (2019, April 22). A History of the Influencer, from Shakespeare to Instagram. Retrieved June 11, 2019, from https://www.newyorker.com/culture/annals-of-inquiry/

Scott, W. A. (1962). Cognitive Complexity and Cognitive Flexibility. *Sociometry, 25*(4), 405.

Segev, S., Fiske, R., & Villar, M. E. (2015). Understanding Bloggers: Opinion Leadership and Motivations to Use Blogs Among Bloggers and Blog Readers. *Marketing Dynamism & Sustainability: Things Change, Things Stay the Same... Developments in Marketing Science: Proceedings of the Academy of Marketing Science,* 123-123.

Shah, D. V., & Scheufele, D. A. (2006). Explicating Opinion Leadership: Nonpolitical Dispositions, Information Consumption, and Civic Participation. *Political Communication, 23*(1), 1-22.

Siebert, A. (1996). *The survivor personality: Why some people are stronger, smarter, and more skillful at handling life's difficulties ... and how you can be, too*. New York, NY: Berkeley Pub. Group.

Skinner, R. (2018). *The Forrester New Wave: Influencer Marketing Solutions,1* (pp. 1-18, Rep.).

Small Introduction to Opinion Leaders - Twitter Research. (2011, May 25). Retrieved June 12, 2019, from https://sites.google.com/site/

Smith, A., & Anderson, M. (2019, April 17). Social Media Use 2018: Demographics and Statistics. https://www.pewinternet.org/

Soldow, G. F. (1982). A Study of the Linguistic Dimension of Information Processing as a Function of Cognitive Complexity. *Journal of Business Communication, 19*(1), 55-69.

Spacey, J. (2018, February 02). 14 Examples of Abstract Thinking. https://simplicable.com/new/abstract-thinking

Spranger, M., Heinke, F., Siewerts, H., Hampl, J., & Labudde, D. (2018). The Eighth International Conference on Advances in Information Mining and Management. In *Opinion Leaders in Star-Like Networks: A Simple Case?* (pp. 33-38). IARIA.

Spreng, R. N., Mckinnon, M. C., Mar, R. A., & Levine, B. (2009). Toronto Empathy Questionnaire. *Journal of Pers Assess, 91*(1), 62-71.

Sripada, C. S. (2013). Simulationist Models of Face-Based Emotion Recognition. *Joint Ventures,* 63-88.

Startup Authority. (2019, May 03). Influencer marketing- How to work with social media influencers in 2019–2 https://medium.com/@startupauthority/

Stephen R. Covey and Keith A. Gulledge, Principle-Centered Leadership, Journal for Quality and Participation, (July/August, 1992) 70-78

Sternharz, N. (2013). *(Nathan of Breslov) Rabbi Natan's Likutey Halakhot: On the four volumes of the Shulchan Arukh*. The Rabbi Israel Dov Odesser Foundation for Printing and Distributing the Works of Rabbi Nachman of Breslov.

Strang, K. D. (2011). Leadership Substitutes and Personality Impact on Time and Quality in Virtual New Product Development Projects. *Project Management Journal, 42*(1), 73-90.

Sudman, S. (1971). Overlap of Opinion Leadership across Consumer Product Categories. *Journal of Marketing Research, 8*(2), 258.

Tan, C.T. & Dolich, I. J. (1979). Cognitive Structure in personality: An investigation of its generality in buying behavior in Olson J. (Ed.) Advances in Consumer Research, 7, 547-551.

The Extraordinary Influence of Ordinary People (2008). Science & Spirit, 19(1), 13.

Time Magazine Staff. (2018, June 28). 25 Most Influential People on the Internet in 2018. Retrieved June 11, 2019, from http://time.com/5324130/most-influential-internet/

Trepte, S., & Scherer, H. (2010). Opinion leaders – Do they know more than others about their area of interest? *Communications, 35*(2).

Tripodi, T., & Bieri, J. (1966). Cognitive complexity, perceived conflict, and certainty. *Journal of Personality, 34*(1), 144-153.

Tsang, A. S., & Zhou, N. (2005). Newsgroup participants as opinion leaders and seekers in online and offline communication environments. *Journal of Business Research, 58*(9), 1186-1193.

Twellow. (2019, June). Twellow.com : Directory of Twitter Users. https://www.searchenginejournal.com/twellowcom-directory-of-twitter-users/7190/

Upfluence. (2019). The Smartest Influencer Marketing Platform. https://upfluence.com/

Vannoy, J. S. (1965). Generality of cognitive complexity-simplicity as a personality construct. *Journal of Personality and Social Psychology, 2*(3), 385-396.

Venkatraman, M. P. (1990). Opinion leadership, enduring involvement and characteristics of opinion leaders: a moderating or mediating relationship? Advances in Consumer Research, Vol 17, 60-67.

Vilponen, A., Winter, S., & Sundqvist, S. (2006). Electronic Word-of-Mouth in Online Environments. *Journal of Interactive Advertising, 6*(2), 8-77.

Waal, F. D. (2009). *The age of empathy: Nature's lessons for a kinder society*. New York: Harmony Books.

Walter, S., & Brüggemann, M. (2018). Opportunity makes opinion leaders: Analyzing the role of first-hand information in opinion leadership in social media networks. *Information, Communication & Society,* 1-21.

Watts, D. J., & Dodds, P. S. (2007). Influentials, Networks, and Public Opinion Formation. *Journal of Consumer Research, 34*(4), 441-458.

Waytz, Adam (2016) The Limits of Empathy, Harvard Business Review

Wefollow. (2019, April). https://twitter.com/wefollow

Weimann, G. (1991). The Influentials: Back to the Concept of Opinion Leaders? *Public Opinion Quarterly, 55*(2), 267.

Weimann, G., Tustin, D. H., Vuuren, D. V., & Joubert, J. P. (2007). Looking for Opinion Leaders: Traditional vs. Modern Measures in Traditional Societies. *International Journal of Public Opinion Research, 19*(2), 173-190.

Weng, J., Lim, E., Jiang, J., & He, Q. (2010). TwitterRank: Finding Topic-sensitive Influential Twitterers. *Proceedings of the Third ACM International Conference on Web Search and Data Mining - WSDM '10.*

Wepman, J. M., & Heine, R. W. (1971). *Concepts of personality*. Chicago: Aldine Publishing Company.

Who Are Influencers? (2018, February 02). www.mavrck.com

Wikipedia: Influencer marketing. (2019, June 13). https://en.wikipedia.org/wiki/Influencer_marketing

Williamson, K. L. (2000, February). *Opinion Leadership*]. In *University of Texas at Austin, Department of Advertising*.

Winter, S., & Neubaum, G. (2016). Examining Characteristics of Opinion Leaders in Social Media: A Motivational Approach. *Social Media Society, 2*(3), 205630511666585.

Winter, S., & Neubaum, G. (2016). Examining Characteristics of Opinion Leaders in Social Media: A Motivational Approach. *Social Media + Society, 2*(3), 205630511666585.

Wyckhuys, K. A., & O'Neil, R. J. (2007). Role of opinion leadership, social connectedness and information sources in the diffusion of IPM in Honduran subsistence maize agriculture. *International Journal of Pest Management, 53*(1), 35-44.

Xu, W. W., Sang, Y., Blasiola, S., & Park, H. W. (2014). Predicting Opinion Leaders in Twitter Activism Networks. *American Behavioral Scientist, 58*(10), 1278-1293.

Yukl, G. (1989). Managerial Leadership: A Review of Theory and Research. *Journal of Management, 15*(2), 251-289.

Zajonc, R. B. (1960). The process of cognitive tuning in communication. *The Journal of Abnormal and Social Psychology, 61*(2), 159-167.

Zajonc, R. B. (1968). Cognitive Theories in Social Psychology. In G. Lindzey & E. Aronson (Authors), *The handbook of social psychology*. New York: Random House.

Zaman, T., Fox, E. B., & Bradlow, E. T. (2014). A Bayesian approach for predicting the popularity of tweets. *The Annals of Applied Statistics, 8*(3), 1583-1611. doi:10.1214/14-aoas741

Zhang, P. (2013). The Affective Response Model: A Theoretical Framework of Affective Concepts and Their Relationships in the ICT Context. *MIS Quarterly, 37*(1), 247-274.

INDEX

S

Social Media, 125, *See Influencers*
Sociograms, 27–28, 42, 93

T

Theory. *See* Personal Construct Theory of Opinion Leadership

Elevator Problem, 40
Hypodermic Needle, 26
Need for Theory, 40
Paradigm Shift, 40
Two-Step Flow, 26
Units of Analysis, 42

Made in the USA
Lexington, KY
23 October 2019